MW00329273

LET'S GO

ONE PHRASE THAT COULD CHANGE YOUR LIFE

JAY MIRALLES

To my wife, Becky, for your encouragement and support. Without you, this book would not have been written. You are my ride or die...

ACKNOWLEDGMENTS

Thank you to all my colleagues and friends who were as excited as I was when I told them about this book. Thank you, Kathy Rygg, for your guidance and helping me find my writer's voice. I have learned so much. Thank you, Kelly Murkins, for the cover design and capturing the energy of this book. Thank you, Van Deeb, for always believing in me, especially when I kept saying that I was going to write this book years ago!

INTRODUCTION

"Let's go!" These are two simple words that embody so much more than just a common phrase. They are words that soldiers have spoken before going into battle, firefighters before entering a burning building, coaches before a big game, family before a wedding ceremony, and doctors before a birth. The words "let's go" are bigger than you and me. "Let's go" is a state of mind, an attitude, a declaration, and a conviction. It's provocative, daring, physical, mental, emotional, and something you feel in your soul. It means always being ready and prepared. It both scares and encourages people. But ultimately, these two words serve as a catalyst for movement and are a promise to yourself to follow through with whatever it is you want to achieve whether large or small.

The phrase "let's go" literally means, let us go, together. You can't "let's go" by yourself. The very definition implies more than one person. No accomplishment is ever achieved without the support of at least one other person, whether it's in the form of modeling someone's behavior or simply reading a book. Often all it takes is for someone to say, "Let's go!" Whether the phrase is yelled or whispered, it just might be enough to get you over that hump—the hump that is your inner voice, which makes you doubt, fearful, and paralyzed to act. The inner voice that says until everything is lined up perfectly, you can't do it. But when someone says, "Let's go!" you don't have time to line up everything perfectly. Being perfect is the enemy of progress.

We live in a world of preparation and planning—to do lists, spreadsheets, white boards, and meetings. But nobody cares about plans in the end. They want to see action, and the only way to separate yourself from others is through action. Be the person who tells others what you're going to do, and then do it. I don't have a special ability or advanced training on taking action. I just know that whenever I've acted upon something, I get results. And the times I've done nothing, I've achieved nothing. We all have dreams and big plans for our lives, but most of us take those plans to the grave because we keep waiting to act on them. But what are we waiting for?

Think about your last accomplishment. What did it entail? What were you scared of before you achieved it? You may not recall saying the words "let's go," but the fact you achieved your goal means you gave yourself permission to do it. Now think of something you wanted to achieve but never did. What prevented you from doing it—fear? Self-doubt? Doubt from others? Time? All of those are the result of what I like to call your inner voice of comfort, which is the enemy of the phrase "let's go." You will never get rid of that inner voice. It's been with you your whole life and knows you. We call this thinking. We have thousands of thoughts every day. How can we approach a problem with fresh ideas when we're burdened with overthinking—a problem that can ultimately hold you back. But I will show you how to recognize it, acknowledge it, and attack it so that you have the clarity to achieve your goals without getting stuck again.

I'm not afraid of the word "failure." I love learning from my mistakes. In fact, mistakes are welcomed. Failure helps you rise to the top and reminds you what sweetness tastes like. I have failed many times on my way to successes. But the biggest failure is inaction. I've wanted to write a book for the past 15 years, but I didn't have the discipline to do it. I also thought I needed to have a perfect plan for it. I finally stopped thinking and planning, borrowed someone else's courage and support, and just gave myself permission to say, "Let's go," and I wrote a book.

People love to just sit and think. We think about what other people think. We think about what others think about us. We are taught to think like everyone else. But nothing ever comes from just thinking. Some people even suffer from analysis paralysis—they input their own facts, variables and outcomes, playing out every scenario possible. I equate it to planning a road trip from Omaha to Denver in which I hesitate to leave unless I know every traffic light I come to along the way will be green. When someone is paralyzed by their thoughts, they won't take action until every condition is right, resources are lined up, and the plan is perfect. If you want to be different, you must take action. You can't let yourself be conditioned by others. You can't let them control your inner voice of comfort. Too many times in my life I've been paralyzed by what others think, what they say, and what I think my worth is to them. Humans tend to crave acceptance, admiration, money, and possessions, but you need to get over those hurdles, which are the result of worrying about what other people think. Instead, you must think autonomously and be able to solve your own problems —you can't rely on others to do it for you. I hope this book helps prepare you to start coming up with your own solutions so you can achieve your goals.

I've seen a lot of great entrepreneurs get to a certain level of success and then become stagnant because they've lost the fire of "let's go." They parade their successes in the form of possessions, which only puts out that fire. Many people subscribe to programs or mentors who give them instructions, but they still fail to go. This book is not a how to, it's a get to—you get to achieve whatever you want. And it doesn't belong to just the intelligent or to the elite. It belongs to everybody, whether you're a college student, a parent, or a business owner. It applies to good situations and bad. The one thing every person has in common who has achieved something is that they aren't just sitting still.

But "let's go" is just the beginning. "Let's go" is not just being brave, having guts, or working through risk. It's being scared and going anyway. It's saying, I may make mistakes, but my intentions are good. It's accepting that you don't have to be perfect. Even if you are the only one on the path, it's important to share your goals. If you don't tell others, you tend not to act on them. When you haven't shared your plan, it's easy to hide behind the comfort of procrastination. But when you say to others, "Let's go!" and they are ready to support you, they become the tribe you are doing it for, whether it's your kids, your employees, or a charity you want to support. The phrase "let's go" gives you permission to be bigger than yourself, and it's the first action item towards success.

I want to help you get closer to your success, whatever that looks like for you. Everybody is looking for something that will bring them happiness. Maybe you're apprehensive and stuck in a moment. Maybe you are trying to get over a big hurdle. Maybe you're trying to solve a small problem. Or maybe you just want more out of life. "Let's go" applies to any situation. And if you're happy and satisfied with your life, then pass this book to someone you know who is stuck or facing a problem.

As we journey together, you will learn how to

identify what it is you want to achieve. You will be able to define your fears, expose them, and uncomplicate your thoughts so you have clarity. You will understand the difference between motivation and discipline and how to structure a discipline so that you crave accountability. You will create a loop so that when you achieve your goal, it will become an addiction that drives you to keep going and achieve more. You will develop a desire to share your successes with others. Finally, you will become a motivation for others to achieve what they want. You will be the one saying, "Let's go!" to your family, friends, and colleagues. You will have the clarity, commitment, and discipline to succeed every time. You will be able to say the one phrase that can change your life.

Ready? 3, 2, 1, let's go!

WHY YOU CAN'T GO

There are a number of reasons that prevent us from saying, "Let's go!" In this chapter we're going to identify the six culprits that are the primary barriers to action: maintaining comfort, adopting narratives, seeking permission, lacking discipline, enabling laziness, and prioritizing possessions. A culprit is someone or something that will rob, sabotage, or ruin your outcome, and the ones discussed in this book are all things that steal from your life. We'll learn how to identify each of these barriers so that we can acknowledge and overcome them. Once you can stand up to these culprits, you will grow, develop, and be on your way to the road of success. It will open a door of endless possibilities and create a new narrative in which you efficiently and effectively say, "Let's go!"

CREATURES OF COMFORT

The first step to any change is identifying the problem. You then have to take ownership and acknowledge the problem. People tend to shift blame to others because it's easier than facing the fact they made a mistake, which is a problem in and of itself. There is only one problem that prevents you from saying, "Let's go!" That problem is you. That problem is me. That problem is all of us, and we need to embrace it. We are all creatures of comfort. We want to protect ourselves from risk, fear, hurt, and failure. We think, plan, and organize to avoid anything that might make us uncomfortable. But all those things are just excuses. They each cater to the inner voice of comfort.

The inner voice of comfort is holding you back from what lies on the other side of risk, fear, and failure, which is unlimited successes. That voice is the one that tells you to put it off until tomorrow, or to not do it at all because you might fail. That voice has been fueled by people and events throughout your life that make you believe you shouldn't go and do. That inner voice fills you with destructive self-talk. It makes you feel safe.

We can't ever get rid of the inner voice of comfort. Rather, the key is to know how to manage it. You must attack the inner voice. You need to be honest with yourself and recognize when that voice is speaking up. Trying to ignore it won't work; not having a relationship with your inner voice of comfort is detrimental to your ability to go. You need to acknowledge the fear it's presenting, but rather than shame or blame yourself, accept the fear and make the decision to go anyway, even if you don't have a perfect plan. When fear or discomfort is present, it's a signal that growth is about to happen!

People who can acknowledge their inner voice of comfort and still go all have one thing in common: they are different from everyone else. Often, we look at celebrities and want what they have. We think they were overnight successes and that we should be too. But then we quickly compare ourselves to them and decide the only way to get there is to be smarter, faster, taller...better. But the only real difference between you and anyone you deem successful, is that they dared to be different, because they overcame their inner voice of comfort and did it anyway.

When I was seven years old, I remember being disciplined by my dad. Afterward, my grandmother said to me, "Your dad means well, he just wants you to do better. And that is only up to you." We are conditioned to think that we must rely on something else to make us better and more successful. But there is no magic pill, or program, or system that will propel you. Luck won't work either. Your biggest enemy when you're stuck in life is your inner voice of comfort. Attacking it implies a relentlessness no matter what that voice says. Once you attack it, you will be able to make a different choice from every other time you've been stuck. You will finally be able to go.

NOT YOUR NARRATIVE

The inner voice of comfort is the result of a lifetime of narratives that we've learned from others: teachers, professionals, politicians, parents, and friends. We are conditioned to believe what others tell us to believe. Everywhere you look someone, or something, is trying to place a narrative on you. TV ads want you to buy their product, politicians want you to adopt their views, and social media teaches you to be like everyone else. We believe in these narratives because we are looking for that quick fix—the product or service that will solve our problem and help us reach the next level. But all those narratives feed the inner voice of comfort. When the product or service doesn't get us where we want to be, then they become excuses, just like the excuses to plan, organize, and think rather than just go and do.

When we listen to other people's narratives and surrender to them, then we end up beating ourselves down. We revert to past pains in life. We reinforce narratives that tell us we can't because we're too old, too young, or not smart enough. They become giants in your mind and will scare you if you let them. Rather than act, we seek comfort behind those narratives. But when you let go of the narratives you've adopted from others over time and create your own, you clear your mind. Having a clear mind paves the way for possibility. Nobody can dampen your dreams when you have clarity. You have to train, develop, and commit to your new narrative. You have to go all in. When you listen to others' opinions, you allow them to shape your thoughts. Eventually these become thought-limiting beliefs.

The best way to combat thought-limiting beliefs is to feed your brain. Pay close attention to what you expose yourself to. Are they feeding your brain? I've found the best way to feed your brain is by reading printed material. When you read, it shuts off your mind to outside things. There is nothing like the basic element of reading. It trains your mind to be disciplined and blocks out chatter. It's impossible to think about other things while you're reading, so it's a great way to clear your mind. A clear mind is necessary in order to attack your inner voice of comfort.

SEEKING PERMISSION

People get stuck in life for different reasons. But the one thing they all have in common is they lack a deeper level of self-awareness. They don't know what they want in life or what their goals really are. If you don't know what you want, someone else will decide for you. I see too many people who want to begin a journey, and they spend all their time doing research and asking for everyone else's opinion. A little of that goes a long way. But the people who succeed are the ones who work in silence. When you start seeking permission from others before taking action, they will poke holes in your ideas, creating fear and doubt, which in turn feeds your inner voice of comfort. Listening to others often prevents us from going at all. But those who choose to go, even if they don't have a perfect plan or approval from everyone, are the ones who dare to be different. You must be the pioneer of your own journey and be a leader of one.

There is a difference between seeking permission and borrowing courage. Seeking permission feeds the inner voice of comfort, whereas borrowing courage is support from someone you trust. When I was young, I wanted to go on my first roller coaster ride at the county fair. My older cousins rode it, and when I saw how excited their faces were when they got off, I wanted to share that excitement too. But my mom told me I was too young. While standing in line for the ride, I started to doubt my decision and tried to talk myself out of going. Then one of my cousins said she would ride with me and told me it would be okay. She gave me her support in the form of borrowing her courage. I felt silly for having doubted my decision. I rode the roller coaster, and when it was over, I yelled, "Let's go again!" Children often have this excitement when they try something new and have success with it. They immediately want to do it again. It's a good reminder for us all.

Asking for permission comes in different forms. Maybe you're looking for validation, acceptance, or a way to get out of doing something. Maybe your insecurity is so strong, you can't see that you're looking for answers you already have but too scared to admit. If you ever catch yourself saying, "I don't know if..." "I don't know when..." "I don't know, but... ." These are all phrases that signal you're seeking permission, which amplifies your inner voice of comfort. Be careful what you ask for, because you will probably get it.

DISCIPLINE DEFICIT

People often think you need to be motivated in order to go. And that's true to a point. Motivation is a great tool that acts as a small spark, but long after the excitement of achievement has faded, discipline is all that remains. Unfortunately, discipline tends to have a negative connotation. It's associated with disciplinary notes, going to the principal's office, or a ruler smacking your hand. I used to visualize a ball and chain or handcuffs when I heard the word "discipline." I associated it with sacrifice, pain, and being in trouble. Now, I consider it an act or behavior you develop that aligns with your values and can be performed without anyone's assistance. But discipline is bigger than something physical. It's stronger than intelligence. It requires digging down deep inside yourself. Discipline involves the basic elements of human survival and leaving all comfort behind, such as eating because you have to in order to survive, rather than eating simply because you want to. Discipline isn't about placing limitations; it's about trimming things out of your life you don't need.

It's being honest with yourself and asking, "Am I doing this for me or for someone else?" You can't practice discipline if you don't believe in the reason you're doing it in the first place. Discipline is not a "quick fix," such as a 90-day program or a get rich quick scheme. It takes hours and hours of practice over time.

Motivation is often found externally. It might be the spark ignited by a presentation, a conversation with a loved one, or even a song. Discipline, on the other hand, comes from within. It cannot be purchased; it must be practiced. Discipline builds habits. It focuses energy and action with intensity and clarity. Discipline can be in the form of a routine that creates a rhythmic pattern to reach or push towards a goal. Discipline helps you remove or run over distractions. Being disciplined implies that your mind has been made up and you've decided to take action regardless of outcome. Discipline helps you separate emotions from physical feelings. It focuses on what is good for us, not what feels good to us. Discipline is not hitting the snooze button when the alarm goes off at 5am. "Let's go!"

Discipline is hitting the gym after a long, tiring day at work. "Let's go!" Discipline is driving past the coffee shop because you're saving money. "Let's go!" Discipline is doing something no matter how much it hurts mentally, no matter how unglamorous or mundane it is. It requires a willpower and effort. When you know you have a task, you must do it. It's incredibly easy to put off discipline, which is procrastination. To put things off until tomorrow feels more comfortable. In fact, procrastination feels so good, it boosts endorphins, which can lead to an addiction to procrastination. Discipline is doing things that make you uncomfortable—a routine you find for yourself. When we see people we admire, it's not the result we are admiring, it's the hard work and discipline they put into it.

When my wife and I were first married, we lived in an apartment. My daughter, Jade, was just over a year old. She was in her crib and had a tiny bug crawling on her. Our living conditions became the motivational spark for me to want better for my family. What followed was not years of continued motivation. The hard work and long hours to pull my family out of that situation was sheer discipline. I faced a lot of disappointment along the way, which made me even more disciplined. I wasn't disciplined because somebody else told me to be but because I told myself to be disciplined. You can't rely on others to practice your discipline. Quick fixes—buying things or leveraging others is a slippery slope and is not discipline. True discipline will cost you everything in terms of comfort, but otherwise it costs you nothing.

I faced another hurdle in my life related to my health. At 237 lbs., I was very unhappy. I had no energy, and my cognitive ability was compromised. I bought everything I could to lose weight: pills, powders, programs, and even injections. Those around me often said, "It's okay, you're fine just the way you are." But I didn't feel fine, and I finally hit rock bottom. I thought I would feel that way forever. And then something clicked—the spark of motivation I needed. I decided to go on the keto diet. Some people told me not to do it. But as soon as I decided I didn't need anyone's permission, that's when I was able to go. Over the course of two years, I lost 70 lbs. Was I motivated along my journey when people complimented how I looked? Of course. It made me temporarily excited, but that motivation only lasted in short bursts. When the motivation wore off, it was discipline that had the strongest impact. It was discipline that made me prepare my meals day in and day out. It was discipline that started to get me massive results. Discipline is obsession and immersion. Discipline means freedom— free from being stuck. Temptation was there every day. Opportunities for procrastination were there every day. But I became so deeply disciplined, I knew I wasn't going to be stopped. Every hurdle I encountered was not enough to stop me. Every time I had a weak moment, I said, "Let's go!"

EASY STREET

Another big barrier to being able to go and achieve a goal is sheer laziness. Everyone has been lazy at one time or another. I still feel lazy at times. We get lazy because it's comfortable, and that contentment continues to make us lazy. Having a steady income, making the next sale, or finally buying the car you've been wanting makes us lazy. Being habitually late for appointments is lazy. Making excuses is lazy. Complaining is lazy. Blaming others is lazy. If all you do is talk about something, you're being lazy. To me, "lazy" is a dirty word. It's a strong beast you must fight. You will stumble, fall, and make mistakes, and it's easy to sit back and sulk. But I don't want to associate myself with lazy people, and you shouldn't either. Laziness is a large barrier to movement. The worst thing you can do is unpack and live in that comfortable spot.

You can't be lazy and be part of the solution. To be part of the solution, you need a little motivation and a lot of discipline. Problem solving requires using the right tools. When people get lazy, they don't want to bother with the right tools. The correct way to hammer a nail into a wall is to use an actual hammer. But some people get lazy, won't go look for a hammer and instead want to just use their shoe. It won't work. If all you want is to take the easy path, you will remain exactly where you're at. Avoid lazy people. Do the work yourself. Don't rely on others to do it for you.

You're going to have many obstacles on the way to becoming disciplined, many of which lead to laziness. The biggest contributors are those thoughts you've been conditioned to believe and have accepted as true: "I'm not good enough," "rich people are bad," "only the educated have access to all that life has to offer." But if you attack those, then you can determine what is really true for yourself. Doing so will help you identify when the beast of laziness is sitting right next to you. Sometimes you can only rely on yourself to get to the next step. Other times, you might need to ask others for help. Asking for help makes us uncomfortable, which is good, because that means it is action. Perhaps you battle depression and need counseling or medication. Maybe you need assistance from an educator or mentor. Asking for help makes you stronger. It humbles you and makes you a better person. Inaction is laziness. I'm afraid of being lazy. I'd rather swear in church than be lazy. If I'm lazy, that means I'm not achieving my goals. And once I achieve my goals, then I'm able to share that achievement with others who can enjoy it with me.

TROPHY TREASURES

One of the biggest problems to "let's go" is tying our achievement to things. Everybody wants to have things: a nice house, a fancier car, a boat, etc. They are often markers of our success. They are also the byproducts of what we seek the most, which is to be recognized by others and viewed a certain way. When you buy a new car, neighbors admire it and congratulate you on it. But what happens if that car were taken away? What are you left with? Do you still feel good about yourself? If you buy a new car and nobody ever sees it but you, would it still make you happy? If the answer is no, then action doesn't fuel you, and you probably aren't being honest about what it is you truly want to achieve. A win doesn't have to be a marker of success, yet we have been conditioned to equate achievement with possessions. But once you've got that end result—that possession—then there is nothing left to keep you going.

If you have a dream to be the wealthiest person on earth, that's okay. Everybody should want to make money. But some of the most successful people are incredibly humble. They don't brag or parade around their wealth. They have defined what wealth truly means to them, and the result is not possessions. It's about the process—why they are doing it and how. It's also about the relationships along the way and impacting the lives of others. You don't admire them for the possessions they have. You admire them for the actions they take. The most successful role models are the ones who are known for what they've contributed to others.

When we focus on trophies—the dream home, the fancy car, the latest and greatest in technology—we don't recognize what we really want to achieve, so we never work on it. Maybe it's spending more time with your family or helping in your community in some way. For me, the real trophy is no trophy. Instead, it's my relationships. Success shouldn't be about what you can get. It should be about what you can give. If you concentrate on what you can give, it will create a loop that reignites "let's go." When your achievements are focused on what's right for you, for your family, and for others, they become a motivation that makes it easier to be disciplined and to keep going long after you've purchased a new house or car. We need to recognize that the things we strive for are just things. But a true accomplishment is something that can never be taken away, and those should be the goals that make you say, "Let's go!"

CHAPTER SUMMARY

We've identified the six primary reasons why we can't go: being comfortable, adopting narratives, seeking permission, lacking discipline, being lazy, and coveting possessions. We should be able to recognize how those barriers present themselves in our everyday lives and why it's critical we push through them. I encourage you to write down every time you encounter one of these barriers. Acknowledge it, but don't dwell in that space. Quickly set it aside so that your mind is clear and ready. In the next chapter, we're going to discover the tools we need handy so that we can pack our bags and go!

3, 2, 1, Let's Go!

What is a narrative you've adopted from someone else? How can you change that narrative?

Do you have a routine that keeps you

disciplined? What is one small thing you can add to that routine?

Are you guilty of focusing on treasures as achievements of your success? What is a better measure of your success?

NOTES

NOTES

2

PACK YOUR BAGS & GO

Now that you can identify the barriers to action and how to attack them, the next step is to arm yourself with all the items you need to pack in your bags so that you're ready to go. In this chapter we will discuss the seven elements needed to achieve your goal: finding a tribe, having something other than work, giving more than you need to, becoming a servant leader, being part of the solution, defining success, and breaking your limitations.

Before you can pack your bags, you need to get into the right mindset for your journey. Since the day you were born, your mindset has been conditioned by your family, friends, competitors, media—anything with which you come into contact. Humans can be easily fooled into thinking that norms are okay. If all of your friends tell you it's impossible to make a six-figure income, you will start to believe it and surrender to that thought. Your natural instinct is to always revert to your default mindset. You can have the most elaborate plan, but when that derails, you will only be as strong as your mindset allows. Like a muscle that needs to be trained and conditioned, you need to train your mindset and feed it powerful thoughts so that it becomes your backbone.

When you're tested, squeezed, or under pressure, do you react, or do you respond? We all react at times—someone disagrees with you, emotions run high, and it usually doesn't have positive results. When you have a strong mindset, you can prepare how to respond to stress. It requires practice so that you can develop a reflex to respond rather than react. Most people with a strong mindset can respond in a calm tone, without yelling, and still make sense. Have you noticed how a seasoned comedian responds calmly when being booed or heckled? It comes from years of practice on stage. When someone reacts, it's the flight or fight instinct kicking in. If there's a fire in your house, your natural instinct is to react by running out of the house. But firefighters have to go against that instinct. They undergo rigorous training so they know how to respond and maintain composure in order to save lives and preserve property—a truly noble act. How will you behave the next time you're under pressure—will you react or respond to the situation?

When was the last time you questioned your mindset and asked yourself when and why you started thinking this way? When we never question the truth, we settle and become complacent and comfortable. We live our lives on cruise control out of convenience. We wait for the automatic doors at a grocery store to open for us. We hold our hands under the faucet in a public restroom, waiting for the water to run. Even when it's not an automatic faucet, we are so conditioned to convenience, we hold our hands under it anyway. We take so many things for granted we no longer know our own mindset. Some people just work hard, pay their bills, and get through life. Others insist there must be more to life and more they can do. I want to challenge you to fight the norm and create a stronger mindset.

Mindset training is an emotional and physical process. Your mindset should go all the way down to your soul. Once you've established a strong mindset, nobody will be able to change it. The emotional process of getting to a strong mindset involves reaching the point where you are happiest, at the highest peak of elation. It's the feeling you get after having a victory and everything you do turns to gold. When your emotions are running high in this positive manner, you are open, unguarded, and attracting good thoughts. Even if small challenges appear, you are easily able to move past them.

But how do you reach that happiness mindset if you feel like a failure and are in your darkest hour? One easy but powerful trick is to listen to music. There is plenty of research available on music's ability to help achieve a great emotional state. It's why athletes wear headphones and listen to music before competing. It sparks emotion. Choose music that is tied to a great time in your life. Concentrate on that moment, feel the emotion, and then free your mind and uplift your thoughts. Once your mind is clear, you can start focusing on your goal.

The physical process of achieving a strong mindset involves movement. You have to physically move to get your mind to change. If you remain hunched over and motionless, your mind will stay stale and you will trap yourself in a dark place. Moving gets your blood pumping and your adrenaline flowing. Something as simple as taking a short walk may be all it takes. We tend to overcomplicate things by trying to have a perfect, foolproof plan before we take action. But all we really need is to put one foot in front of the other. The emotional and physical processes are good on their own. But when you combine them—taking a walk while listening to music—you achieve that strong mindset. Once your mindset is in a strong state of clarity, then you are ready to pack the next seven items in your bags and begin your journey.

FIND YOUR TRIBE

We're all familiar with the concept that you are the sum of the five people you are around the most. Who do you spend time with? Who do you go to for advice? Do you seek advice from people you want to be like? Or do you seek advice from only those who will give you their approval? Often, we simply seek advice as a way to fish for compliments and soothe our egos. But you don't need others' opinions of yourself. If that's all you want, you might as well live their life, not yours.

The tribe I seek advice from includes people I'm sometimes uncomfortable around, but they bring perspectives from very different points of life. I ask them for the truth, not simply what I think is right. If all you want is to *feel* better, then you can read a self-help book. But if you want to *be* better, then you need to open yourself up to honest feedback and even criticism. Being better requires action. You can gain all the knowledge required to be better—even become a subject matter expert—but until you put it into action, you won't be any better. Remember, discomfort is an indicator of growth. We like to keep friends out of convenience. And although it's important to have a support network, sometimes your friends can put rose-colored glasses on your eyes because they don't want to hurt your feelings. Or they allow you to complain, or they complain to you. If that's the case, it may be time to find some new members for your tribe.

When you seek out new members for your tribe, are you just "picking someone's brain," or are you truly trying to gain insight into your own life? When people claim they want advice but already have decided on a solution, they aren't really open to anything new. Often the best approach is to simply listen and watch a mentor's actions. Avoid the mistake of taking from your tribe and not contributing to it. It's toxic to fixate on "what's in it for me." Instead, focus on finding mentors for your tribe who are great examples, such as parents, business owners, neighbors, or coaches. Spend your time with those people instead of wasting it on the wrong people. A good friend of mine said, "Time is finite, and you can't spend all your time with everybody." Time is one of your most valuable resources. When it comes to your tribe, guard your time and invest it well.

BEYOND YOUR JOB

I used to think that work, work, work, and then more work would get me ahead. But every time I only worked and did nothing else, I experienced burnout. When you have nothing in your life except work, you can get stuck, unable to see solutions through the stress. You must have something other than work. I once believed that hobbies had to generate income. I thought that every minute of my time had to equal a dollar. But the best hobbies are ones that make no money and instead simply generate purpose.

Creative outlets always bring new ideas. It's why adult coloring books became popular. Mindless activities help relieve stress and bring you clarity. Have you ever lost your sunglasses and can't find them when you're stressed and frantically looking? Then a day later when you're not thinking about it, you finally stumble upon them. If you are consumed with always making your next buck, you will always be chasing your tail. In order to succeed, you must have an outlet other than work.

It could be playing cards with friends, exercising, or a woodworking project. It also includes going on vacation, which is important for two reasons. First, a vacation allows you to celebrate your successes. Second, a vacation allows you to truly separate yourself from work. Society glamorizes grinding and hustling—what does it even mean? Working eight days a week? Something that causes you pain? If grinding and hustling feels painful and makes you angry, then is it really what you should be doing? Have you ever felt guilty for going on vacation and not being available at your job? Instead of completely unplugging, you still check emails and voicemails in case your biggest client needs you. But you can't be held captive by any one person, or think you're so important that your company will fall apart if you don't respond to that email right away. Rather than succumb to demands of society, set yourself up for success even with your vacations by creating an infrastructure. Turn on autoresponders for your email. Forward your calls to a colleague. Tell those around you that you'll be on vacation with your family. If they don't understand, they shouldn't be in your tribe. And remember the goal is not just to earn a living but to make a life.

GIVE MORE

Two years ago, I had an acquaintance who was struggling with their health. They were angry at life and not looking for help. But I called and left a simple message of hope. They never responded. Then out of the blue I received a text message from that person saying how my message had impacted their life and they had finally lost weight. It wasn't just my message. The person said they had watched my actions over social media, at events, and through other friends, which ultimately led them to take action. Simply telling someone they can do it will not spark them into action, but believing they can model their behavior after yours, will. That text message was the most pleasant surprise. It reminded me how important it is to give more than you need to give. People always remember how you made them feel, and you will always be known for the impact you made.

When you give more than you need to, you truly connect with those around you. People are impressed with doing a little extra, especially these days. It might require a little more effort, but it goes a long way. Going above and beyond to serve your customer, client, or community doesn't require much. Why do people go to a particular coffee shop or grocery store? It's not usually because it's the least expensive option—often it's quite the opposite—but it's because of the little extras in the form of customer service they receive. Being a leader also means giving just a little more. It doesn't require money, it just requires an accountability to follow through, or to be a group's cheerleader. Giving a little more never hurt anybody. Growing up, my siblings and I were always taught to give away the first piece, the first sip, or the last bite.

That always stuck with me. To this day I try to do little things, such as inviting someone else to speak first or to take the last chair. When you give more than you need to, the byproduct is that you are noticed and remembered—you make an impact.

In fact, the people you tend to gravitate toward are usually those who give extra and *are* just a little "extra." Have you ever wondered why they give so much? I guarantee it's not so they can get something in return. And they certainly don't have to have a lot to give a lot. Giving more than you need to requires character, integrity, and follow through. Perhaps it's because they're successful and want to give so they can spread their success. After all, you can't give what you don't have. It's not the promise of giving. It's when you don't say anything, but simply do something extra— something a little more thoughtful and intentional. As a society we tend to do what's required and nothing more. We use excuses such as "I'm tired," or "it's not my job." Hearing those words should burn a little hole in your soul and make you determined not to be that way.

The best examples of giving more are the ones where you're not publicizing it. When I give someone a gift or card, I prefer they don't open it in front of me. Instead, I want them to have their own private space so they can have a genuine reaction and not a potentially forced response. If what I gave made an impact, I will know later. You shouldn't give more to be recognized. You should give more to be impactful. Poisonous giving is expecting something in return, outdoing someone else's giving, or bragging about your giving. You can publicize what you're passionate about, but don't publicize when you've given more than you need to. Some of my greatest accomplishments have come from giving more when nobody knows about it, and I'm the only one who sees the result and the impact.

Giving extra is not about money, time, or a specific cause. It's about stretching a little outside of your comfort zone. Giving extra often comes in the form of helping people who help others. It might involve recruiting volunteers, identifying talent, or simply encouraging other leaders. My parents always taught me to give more than I needed to, even during times when they had nothing. Mother Teresa had nothing and gave the world everything. The richest people leave behind a legacy, not money. Even Dr. Maya Angelou said, "No one has ever become poor from giving."

SERVANT LEADERSHIP

One of the things nearest and dearest to my heart is servant leadership. Even before I knew what it was called, I practiced servant leadership. I first learned the word "leadership" when I was in the military. It meant structure and rank. Servant leadership is the ability to lead others regardless of rank, social disposition, net worth, title, or education level. It's a universal language recognized by everyone. It doesn't need to be taught to be observed. Some of the best fighters in the military weren't the highest ranking. They were the ones who volunteered to go first and put themselves in harm's way, much like firefighters and police officers. But servant leaders also include the mom who has a job, cooks, cleans, home schools during a pandemic, and puts her entire family ahead of herself unselfishly.

The simplest things can show servant leadership, such as leading a small group at church, picking up litter in the street during your morning run, or waking up early to accomplish things at home before everyone else's day starts. Being a servant leader is not about giving other people orders. It's about setting an example for others to follow. Servant leaders take ownership and accept responsibility for the situation or outcome. They have a high level of perception and use their experience to bring results in any situation. A servant leader doesn't mean you have to be meek, less than, or submissive—there's no rank to servant leadership. It simply means in order to serve others, you put them before yourself. And when you serve others selflessly, they feel it, which creates a bond of trust for what you're trying to accomplish.

A servant leader could be anyone in any organization, not just a CEO or team captain. It simply has to be someone who is willing to step up and push the group in the right direction. Sometimes other people think this takes too much work or time, but something magical happens when a servant leader steps up, and it's awesome to watch those people in action.

Everybody knows a leader and many aspire to be one. Too often we associate being a leader with holding a certain position in an organization, such as president or general manager. And our inner voice of comfort usually tells us we could never hold one of those positions. But it's not the position that makes them a leader, it's their characteristics, and that's what we want to see in ourselves. A true servant leader is willing to be a pioneer, on the front line, and willing to make mistakes. They are a little bolder than the rest. They will always break through the rhetoric of "we've always done it this way." When others get stuck on process, the servant leader helps the group move past the obstacle. As a servant leader, I'm often impatient when I see a group stewing over a problem. It takes just one person to make a decision and say, "Let's go!"

BE PART OF THE SOLUTION

If you're not part of the solution, you're part of the problem. Destructive behavior comes in many forms, but the simplest is in the form of complaining and doing nothing about it. It's easy to complain about something. Being part of the solution is asking the question, "if it's not possible now, how do we make it possible?" Most of our problems are ones we create for ourselves to make us feel better about our inadequacies and failures. If you've ever thought, "how come I didn't win that award?" or "I'm nicer than they are," then you are part of the problem. When you complain, *you* are the one who suffers and doesn't grow or become better.

Have you ever been stuck listening to someone complain? Maybe you were the one doing the complaining? When you participate in the complain game, everyone loses. When you engage in complaining, it makes you part of the problem. When you complain to others, what makes you think they won't in turn complain about you? Do you have constant complainers in your life? Why do they have a place in your tribe? I want to separate myself from complainers. They don't want you to help solve their problems, they just want you to listen. A complaint is presenting a problem without wanting a solution. People who complain usually have an inability to problem solve. Can you go through an entire day avoiding complainers? Be aware of them because they are always part of the problem.

Being part of the solution requires putting yourself second. You must admit you don't know all the answers but are willing to ask for help. We don't want to risk being judged or say something dumb in front of a group. But being part of the solution means being vulnerable and sometimes unpopular with the masses. You must swallow your pride and have an open mind and self-awareness that you don't know everything. You also can't rely on a quick fix. You don't need to seek approval, but you do need to seek answers from others. Those who are part of the solution are often surprised by the answers they find.

If you want to be part of the solution, never settle. You must always think beyond what is right in front of you. I teach my children that they don't need to be the smartest math or English student, they just need to learn how to think critically for themselves. If I always give them the answer, then they will always wait for the solution to come to them. If my son forgets his football helmet, he has to sit out for the entire game. But that's a problem he needs to solve for himself. I don't bring him his helmet and solve it for him. As parents we get caught up in not wanting to be unfair to our kids. We want to be good to them, but we need to be good *for* them. If you constantly solve their problems and cater to their every need, then they will always be part of the problem and not the solution. Some children are great at solving problems. They are true mavericks, always asking questions and being creative. As adults, we can learn a lot from those types of kids.

Similar to parents and their children, the best companies are the ones that empower their employees to find their own solutions, not solve everything for them. The business with a CEO who doesn't encourage their employees to share ideas, risks bankruptcy. There are many examples of CEOs who didn't make new solutions for the changing times, customer demand, or adapt products to a new audience. Being part of the solution is asking questions and posing challenges that team members can solve for themselves, even if that question is, "how can you do better next time?" You must become a better conversation starter and learn how to ask powerful, open-ended questions. Do you want to know what people are interested in? Ask them. Do you want to know what's important to someone? Ask them. You don't have to be a detective or an investigative journalist, you just have to learn how to ask questions in the right way and have genuine interest in people. Problem solving is a critical skill that requires asking good questions so you can gather good data.

If you need some inspiration, just watch Shark Tank. There are new solutions to problems being created by people every day. Those are the people who don't just accept what is visible right in front of them. They asked questions to find a better answer and be part of the solution.

DEFINING SUCCESS

The word "success" has different meanings to different people. We have been conditioned to believe that success is an expensive ring for winning the Super Bowl, being the first-place contestant on *Jeopardy*, or the Dow Jones being at an all-time high. We've already established in Chapter One that material things don't equal success. You are the only person who can define what success means to you. A good guideline to help you define success is anything that makes you happy, gives you time to pause and enjoy, and shares what you've gained with others. For me, success is about self-reliance and knowing I have the ability to create anything I want and to get through any situation. It's not just one thing but a culmination of things that add to the enhancement of my life. I like to view success in varying degrees. Having a successful day means I've invested time in my marriage, have given my children my undivided attention, and have been purposeful with my whole family. Success today was putting these words to paper in a meaningful way that hopefully inspires you. Success might also mean working on a long-term project that others said wouldn't work, but we finished it anyway. Success is not the money that was attained at the end of the goal. It's that I was able to accomplish it in spite of those who said it couldn't happen. I had the knowledge and the experience to influence the outcome. That to me is success. It sounds simple, but true success has a big impact on those around you.

I like the phrase, "you can't hitch a U-Haul to a hearse." At the end of the day, you can't take your possessions with you, so you need to live your life not for money and things but to be purposeful. Too often we equate success with things that soothe us momentarily or get us to the next thing. While researching success, I found many different definitions. I even asked others for their definition of success. But success is the result of simply doing things for the right purpose and with the right intention. If you do that, then success is the natural byproduct. Success lies in the impact of sharing what you have for the betterment of others, whether that is money, influence, time, or the ability to connect people. I know that even if I completely run out of money, I can still share by volunteering, teaching, and connecting people for the greater good.

BREAK LIMITATIONS

Every time you think you can't do something, you are placing limitations on yourself. It's often difficult to realize that's what you're doing, but thought-limiting beliefs are in all of us. They are part of our conditioning, and we constantly give others permission to limit us. Sometimes it's labeled as "protecting you." Parents can be some of the first people who give you thought-limiting beliefs. When a child says, "I want to be a professional athlete," how many parents tell them they better have a Plan B for when it doesn't work out? Or an adult who wants to start a business and is immediately told that most businesses fail in the first 24 months? If you always have a Plan B, then you will settle for it. The people who give you these thought-limiting beliefs aren't trying to be mean. They genuinely don't want you to be disappointed or see you get hurt. But isn't part of growth and success emotional and sometimes physical pain? If you go through life comfortable, then you'll only get what you've always had. For those who want more, it's okay to fall down, be disappointed, and get hurt, because it means you've taken a chance. Accepting the norm is one of the fastest ways to keep you stuck in place. As a leader, when you allow your team to stay in its current state, then you show you have no interest in developing them. Instead, your job is to challenge them and help foster ideas for solutions. If you don't let people think for themselves, then you must not need them in the first place.

Playing it safe will never change your thought-limiting beliefs. Accepting that things are "just the way they are" is the worst thought-limiting belief. Humans naturally want to be in a homogeneous state of being where our lives aren't interrupted by opposing forces that cause us to take risks. That's why it's so much easier to believe the thoughts of "you can't" or "you shouldn't." The eight hours you work at your job are fine, but you should be working on yourself the other eight waking hours of your day. If there's one thing you should bet on, it's yourself. Others may float in and out of your life and help a little here or there, but you can't rely solely on them. You have to believe in yourself so much, that when an obstacle gets in your way, it won't bother you. Instead, you will find a way to move over, around, or through it.

Thought-limiting beliefs are actually tied to the inner voice of comfort and lead to laziness and complacency. Some of the best examples of innovation are the ones that overcame thought-limiting beliefs, such as taking six tons of metal and making it fly through the air. Now we can't imagine life without airplanes. Too many people accept thought-limiting beliefs and go through life as sheep, following other people's agendas. But we don't have to be sheep. Take the lion's mentality and ask, "How can I achieve this in spite of everything?" Every success you've had in life was at first opposed by a thought-limiting belief. It was signaled by fear, doubt, and anxiety. But once you reached the other side of those feelings, you found success. The next time you feel those same emotions, recognize it as a signal that something big is about to happen. Despite those limiting beliefs, look in the mirror and say, "Let's go!"

CHAPTER SUMMARY

Once you get into the right mindset physically and emotionally to begin your journey, then you can pack your bags so you're ready to go. You will need to find a tribe, have something other than work, give more than you need to, become a servant leader, be part of the solution, define success, and break your thought-limiting beliefs. You should now be able to define each one of these, determine what each means for you, and then have the clarity of mind and confidence that you can incorporate them as you move forward. If at any point you forget one, don't abandon your journey! Instead of giving up and reverting back to your inner voice of comfort, recognize the setback and refocus. Believe in yourself, re-pack your bag, and push forward. Remember that mistakes result in progress.

Next, we're going to dive into what you need to get going!

3, 2, 1, Let's Go!

Who do you consider to be your tribe? Is there anyone who isn't a good fit within that group? Who would you like to add to your tribe?

What hobbies do you have besides work? Is there an activity you'd like to try?

How do you serve others? Is there a cause you'd like to get involved with?

NOTES

NOTES

WHAT YOU NEED TO GET GOING

Once you have all the elements we discussed in Chapter Two packed into your bag, there is one vital element still needed in order to go: energy. We all learned in science class that energy can neither be created nor destroyed. It's either stored, working, or wasted—in other words, expended or invested. Energy is also available in a finite amount, which means you can't create new energy. In this chapter we're going to dive deeper into the concept of energy flow, the importance of being aware of it, and how that relates to being able to go.

ENERGY FLOW

Where does your energy flow? An easy way to determine that is to look at your daily calendar and your bank account. How are you spending your time? What are you spending your money on? That is where your energy is focused. A lot of people aren't aware of where they focus their energy, resulting in wasted efforts, either through a lack of thought or no thought at all. People either sit idle for too long or they run at 150 mph. When it comes to energy flow, you must be responsible with the energy you have and put it to good use.

PHYSICAL ENERGY FLOW

Energy flows through us physically in the form of our health. In any given day, you only have so much energy with which to take care of yourself. So, you must set aside time every day to maintain your health by having a good routine, developing good dietary habits, and getting enough rest and sleep. If you don't plan that into your day, then it makes the tasks in front of you more difficult. It's no different than having to spread mulch in your yard. It would be a waste of energy to move it one shovelful at a time. Instead, you plan ahead and know that you need a wheelbarrow to make better use of your time and energy. Everyone has some degree of physical demand that is needed daily to perform their tasks at hand, so you must be in optimal health to be able to expend that energy. Most people take this energy for granted until it's temporarily taken away, such as when you're sick or injured. But being mindful of the finite amount of energy you have helps ensure you are using that flow toward maintaining your physical self, which is good energy management.

FINANCIAL ENERGY FLOW

Energy is all around us, but the ability to harness it and use it solely for good, especially financially, isn't always easy. We subconsciously waste effort and time because we don't value our energy. You work hard at your job day after day. The energy you use to work is transferred in the form of money—your paycheck. It's important not to waste that transformed energy on a frivolous purchase. If you work hard for every dollar you earn, then don't be tempted to waste it on things you don't need. Instead, think about how you can take that money—a form of energy—and put it to work for you in a productive way. You will know it's productive and a good flow of financial energy because it moves you toward your goal and what you have defined as success for yourself.

TRANSFER OF ENERGY FLOW

Another form of energy flow is the transfer of energy between two people. Whenever two people meet, there is always a transfer of energy—one person gives more and the other takes more. This is a natural process and can be beneficial. For example, the energy transfer might be emotional, such as giving someone a feeling of hope, joy, or motivation. But it may also be detrimental, such as someone taking energy from you by having a bad attitude or wasting your time by complaining. Having energy doesn't necessarily mean you have to be the most enthusiastic person in the room. It's more about being aware of the energy you are both giving and taking.

When I think of the word energy, I think of focus. Business Strategist Tony Robbins said, "Where focus goes, energy flows." Not being aware of your energy has unintended consequences, both good and bad. When you aren't aware of your energy flow, then it becomes diluted. Think of the sun. Under normal circumstances, its rays are diluted. But when those rays are focused through a magnifying glass, they are so concentrated they can actually start a fire. Similarly, when our energy and efforts are being expended in ten different directions that aren't congruent with our goals, then those efforts are diluted and it becomes wasted energy. But when we focus our energy and transfer it to others, especially in a positive way, then the results can ignite and have a big impact.

TIMING OF ENERGY FLOW

Energy is rhythmic. It relies on timing. Energy flows in waves, and when someone or something disrupts that wave, it results in a poor outcome. That's why you can't force your energy onto people, projects, or plans. You have to be aware of the impact your energy can have, both positive and negative. Think of playing jump rope as a child. The two people turning the rope get into a rhythm along with the jumper. They become synchronized, with energy flowing equally among them. Then a fourth person decides to run in without a single thought, and it messes up the flow for everyone—the jumping stops. When you impart your own energy without regard to the existing energy, then you run the risk of having a negative impact on the overall flow. But when you are aware of your own energy, and both give and take equally, then you will be able to have positive, meaningful collaboration. It will result in moving forward and contributing to the greater good to succeed.

You also don't want to disrupt energy flow just because you think your ideas are better, or if you do all the work yourself, you'll get better results. There are Little League baseball coaches who are more concerned about teaching kids the game than winning, whereas other coaches don't care about a good learning environment because they only care about winning. Both coaches are expending the same amount of energy, but one is for the good of the kids and the other is for the good of the coach. When expending your energy is self-serving, that's when energy disrupts the flow. Even world leaders have to manage flows of energy. Do the leaders you admire sacrifice their own agenda for the good of many, or do they sacrifice the good of many for their own agenda? Take a close look at your own energy flow and whether or not you are using it for the good of many. If you're not, it may be beneficial to look at the timing of your energy flow.

MEASURING ENERGY FLOW

Unfortunately, our bodies aren't equipped with gauges and meters to measure energy levels. So, you have to be able to measure your energy level for yourself. It'd be nice if we had a scale of 1-10, or were able to measure energy remaining like a character in a video game. But measuring energy is so different for everyone, it requires a lot of inward reflection and insight. You consciously know when you have more energy on certain days than others. But how do you measure it? I like to measure my energy by the good I'm able to share that makes an impact. As a realtor, this may mean that I have to perform ten tasks that day in order to help my client submit an offer on their dream home. In order to do that, I know that I must have the right mindset, I must feed my body correctly, and I must be prepared so that my flow of energy isn't interrupted. Some days my energy level is higher than others. While it's okay and normal to have some low energy days, if you have too many, your efforts will lack and your health will deteriorate. You also can't give energy you don't have, or you end up disappointing people. This could be in the form of missed appointments, empty promises, or simply not being "present" when around others. This can all be avoided by having an awareness of your energy level and what you need in order to perform at your best. Then you must go one step further and make sure those needs are being met every day and you're not wasting your energy on other things.

A smile is the simplest form of energy that makes an impact. It is the easiest way to transfer your energy to someone else. With a simple smile, people can see, hear, and feel your energy, and that transfer of energy is contagious. When someone with energy walks into a room and transfers that energy to you, it lifts you up. But when someone else walks into a room with negative energy, it can instantly cause anxiety and suck the life out of the room. Being prepared is one of the best ways to combat low energy. When you wake up an hour late, your routine—the timing of your energy flow—is disrupted. Waking up late can make your entire day out of sync. That's low energy flow. Are you always running late? Always trying to play catch up? That's lack of routine impacting your energy. When you have focus and purpose, then your energy has focus and purpose. Your purpose should be so clear that you are aware of how your actions are going to be carried out based on the energy you have. And all those actions and energy should be flowing in the right direction, for good, toward your goals.

CHAPTER SUMMARY

The concept of energy flow is important to understand as it relates to accomplishing your goals. You must be aware of how and where your energy is flowing, especially with regard to your health and your finances. Make sure the energy for both is flowing toward your goals. You must also be aware of how energy is transferred between people, both negatively and positively. Don't let negative people or activities disrupt your energy flow. Being able to recognize the timing of energy flow and how it can impact an outcome is important. Remember that when contributions are for the greater good, then timing can lead to harmony. But when contributions are self-serving, then timing can lead to sabotage. And finally, being able to measure your own energy—honestly—is a critical skill. It helps you determine the energy level needed to perform tasks that result in positive outcomes over and over again, not just for yourself, but especially for those around you. "Let's go!"

3, 2, 1, Let's Go!

Where does your energy currently flow? Do your efforts go toward your health? Finances?

Who or what disrupts your energy flow? How can you prevent it from happening again?

Do you focus your energy on activities that serve the greater good? If not, how can you change it so they do?

NOTES

NOTES

4

HOW TO KEEP GOING

Now that you have an understanding of energy flow as it relates to getting going, the next step is to address each of the elements of energy needed in order to *keep* going. In this chapter we'll discuss the topic of energy management. It serves as an umbrella under which numerous concepts fall: being a conductor versus a resistor, insulation versus isolation, connecting to a power grid, having an energetic attitude, avoiding a short circuit and potential energy crisis, conserving your energy, wasting energy, switching your energy on and off, unplugging from the power grid, making energizing connections, and how to be energy efficient. We'll discuss each of these concepts and how they all relate to managing your energy so that you can keep going in order to accomplish your goals over and over again.

ENERGY MANAGEMENT

As we discussed in the last chapter, everything you do requires energy, and managing your energy flow is critical to any success. As we discuss each concept in this chapter, I want you to visualize yourself as a power plant. At a power plant, every employee must be conscious of where the energy is flowing. It must all flow in the right direction and to the right places in order to produce a good output. We must manage ourselves like a power plant and constantly be conscious of our energy, where it's flowing, and what outcomes it's producing. Each of the next sections will examine a different aspect necessary in order to provide the best energy management for your personal power plant so that you can keep your energy flowing and keep going.

CONDUCTOR VS. RESISTOR

A conductor as it relates to energy is something that connects two elements together. There's a transfer of energy when you have a conductor. Think about how you interact with people. Do they regularly seek you out for help or advice? Do they ask you to join their groups or work on their projects? Do they ask you for input? If the answer is yes, then you are a conductor. People are attracted to the energy that flows out of you. They want to be around you and value your influence.

If you don't fit into the above category, is it because

you tend to resist change? Does it make you uncomfortable when things don't fall under the norm? Do you poke holes in other people's plans or ideas? Do you think your methods are always better than others? Do you enjoy playing "devil's advocate?" If you answered yes to any of these, then you are a resistor who doesn't let energy flow. Resistors don't like change, and dare I say it, are happy with where they are at in life.

In business, a company is only as strong as its greatest resistor. Imagine a small business with nine employees. Eight of those employees are enthusiastic and open to new ideas, but one employee resists change, is skeptical, and at times unprofessional. That employee is the weakest link, or resistor. As a business owner you must either correct or remove them in order to let the energy flow among the other conductors. If you feel like you aren't succeeding at work, really examine yourself and make sure you aren't acting as a resistor and cutting off your energy either from yourself or going towards others. It's never too late to become a conductor and refocus your energy to move you forward toward success.

INSULATION VS. ISOLATION

Similar to conductor and resistor, insulation and isolation are opposites. Insulation is a protective barrier, whereas isolation completely removes something from its environment. Insulation can be very helpful in managing energy and examines how you place yourself among other people. Sometimes it's necessary to insulate, or put some space between you and others or their ideas in order to make sure your energy continues to flow in the right direction. You may need to insulate yourself from negative people and ideas to allow room for positive people and ideas. You can insulate yourself while still interacting with people, just make sure you are interacting with the *right* people. Sometimes we need to insulate ourselves in order to preserve or recycle our energy. Having down time for self-care is important, and sometimes you have to insulate yourself for a short time in order to do that.

Isolation, on the other hand, is completely cutting yourself off from others and not interacting with anyone at all. When people routinely expose themselves to negativity, they can become depressed and stop their flow of energy. Either consciously or unconsciously they think the only solution is to completely isolate from the outside world. This puts them in an unhealthy place. Isolation is a mistake because it stops all energy flow. I worry about people who isolate themselves, and you should too. They often have no support and don't even want the energy of others. Although it's important to protect yourself from negativity, you don't want to insulate yourself to the point of isolation and become unhealthy. However, there is hope for isolated people by connecting them to the power grid.

THE POWER GRID

The entire world is a power grid. Life is a power grid. We are all connected in some way via our power grid. You are connected to your family, to your friends, to your co-workers, and to your community. You are connected to the city you live in, both the good and the bad aspects of it. You can be 22 miles apart from someone and still be connected. When one person on the grid expends energy, it has a ripple effect. For example, if you expend energy in the form of a purchase at a retail store, that energy—in the form of money—is transferred to the store owner, who invests that money into the business either to hire a new employee or expand their products offered.

Because we are all connected by the power grid, it's especially important to be mindful of our energy flow. Most people are focused on expending their energy for positive purposes, attracting good people to them, and giving back in some way. But there are also takers on the power grid. They want your money and time without bothering to ever give back. Those people often think they are above the power grid and the rules of energy flow don't apply to them. But maintaining the balance of the power grid is important to its overall success. So, you need to be aware of everything and everyone around you; every thought, decision, and action you take affects the power grid and everyone connected to it. And for those who have isolated themselves, there are plenty of people on the power grid ready and willing to provide professional help. That's one of the beautiful aspects of the human power grid—there is always someone who can direct their energy toward helping others.

ENERGETIC ATTITUDE

When you want to make a big impact, it requires a lot of energy. The last time you listened to a motivational speaker, did they just sit on stage and talk quietly? Or did they move while they spoke with energy and enthusiasm? Did that energy motivate you? Did it leave a lasting impact and make you want to incorporate changes into your life or career? Having an energetic attitude is necessary in order to go, especially if you're trying to get a group to all go with you.

If you are working with a team of 20 people on a project, how do you make an impact? Do you sit quietly in the room while others discuss ideas? Do you look at your phone instead of being present and engaged? Do you sit with your arms crossed, giving off a stressed, negative vibe? Or do you smile, ask questions, and contribute ideas? Even if you are stressed, you can still approach a problem in a positive way when you have an energetic attitude. Your attitude and how others perceive your attitude will influence every task you are involved with. Being able to manage your energy and knowing when to have an energetic attitude and when to temper it are important skills.

We live in a society where multi-tasking is

celebrated and encouraged. People are obsessed with having multiple plates spinning and wishing to achieve many goals. Although that's generally positive, we know you only have a finite amount of energy in a day. When we use too much energy on excitement, bouncing from one task to the next, then we quickly use up our energy. We must learn to manage our energy and know when to dial down the energetic attitude in order to focus on a task at hand, and when to dial the energetic attitude up to transfer our energy to others and motivate them to move forward.

We must all choose when to have an energetic attitude and what causes us to have that attitude. I may be excited about the thought of buying a new car, but is that in line with my current goals? Should I be expending my energy by searching online for cars all day, or should I be focusing my energy on tasks that relate directly to my long-term financial goals?

Should I be focusing my energetic attitude on the person who is a resistor or the person who is a conductor? Sometimes when we encounter a resistor, we try to use our energetic attitude to influence them. But often this is not a good use of energy. It usually takes our focus away from our goals and ends up with poor results. Having the right attitude at the right time and transferred to others appropriately will always end with better results.

Humans constantly seek out energy and absorb the energy around us. When you are aware of your energy level and attitude, then you can adjust it as needed. This requires practice, patience, and being honest with yourself. Energy always begins with your mindset. Your mindset controls your attitude. And your attitude is what helps you be positive, upbeat, and resilient so that it's easier for energy to flow and transfer to those around you. Too often I see people who tell themselves they need to keep going in order to take care of everyone else's needs. They force an energetic attitude on everyone in an effort to keep going. An example is a parent who takes on all the responsibility for the family and the household. They aren't honest about their energy level and end up neglecting their own needs—not managing their energy. When this happens over and over again, then it leads to problems such as resistance, isolation, and short circuiting.

SHORT CIRCUIT

A short circuit occurs when there is a surge of energy. It's easy to short circuit yourself, and it happens every day. A lot of times you aren't even aware when it happens. The reason it can be so difficult to recognize is because most of the time it happens with good intentions. It occurs when we want the best for ourselves and for others. We want to please people, help people, and see them succeed. We thrive on the immediate satisfaction of giving others our energy. Unfortunately, constantly putting our energy into others—power surges—will result in becoming out of balance. When our energy is out of balance, we short circuit.

Have you ever over promised and under delivered? Perhaps you were too energetic about taking on a project and made a promise to meet an unrealistic deadline. That deadline comes and goes and you don't deliver, leaving a feeling of shame. Your intentions were good, but in the end you short circuited yourself. I can think of many situations when I short circuited by promising something in the moment. Looking back, I knew it would be difficult to deliver on that promise, but I did it anyway. Not only was I not honest with myself up front, but I didn't have the right tribe in place to help keep me accountable. Now I make sure that I surround myself with a tribe that prevents me from short circuiting. When I make an enthusiastic promise, they serve as a reminder to manage my energy and keep the flow focused in the right direction to achieve the goal at hand.

ENERGY CRISIS

Some people get into a habit of short circuiting. When this happens over and over again, you can quickly fall into an energy crisis. You can recognize these people because they are always running like their hair is on fire. They jump from one idea to the next, trying to accomplish everything on their own with a "I can do it all" attitude. That mentality should be a red flag signaling a potential energy crisis.

An energy crisis is the lack of controlling energy flow. You are not consciously managing nor transferring your energy. You are taking on responsibilities that could be shared by others, but you feel you can't "trust" anyone else to do the tasks. High achievers tend to fall subject to an energy crisis because they don't want to ask for help. Unlike short circuiting, an energy crisis can last a long time. You probably aren't aware when you're in one, yet those around you can easily see it. If you get comments that "you look tired" or "you need some time off" then you are probably experiencing an energy crisis.

You can't be in an energy crisis for an extended period of time without suffering consequences. You may experience mental health issues, physical health issues, or your relationships may deteriorate. Nobody intends to fall into an energy crisis; rather, they are expending energy to a fault, and it ends up being a detriment to themselves. I'm a doer who has many things going on at once. I thrive on motivation, investing in myself, and always want to take on the world's problems. Because this is my personality, I know I have to be careful and mindful about expending too much energy trying to do too much, either on my own or for others. Sometimes it requires admitting you can't do it all, being humble, brave, and asking for help.

It may also require not expending too much energy on helping someone else out of an energy crisis. In that case, referring them to an energy partner, or professional, such as a counselor, physician, coach, or mentor, might be the best way to help them and prevent your own energy crisis. For example, if you have a friend going through a divorce, they may be in an energy crisis and expending a lot of energy confiding in you. Although it may be your natural tendency to always listen and try to help, the best advice might be to refer them to a counselor. That way, you insulate yourself, manage your own energy flow, and prevent a short circuit or energy crisis of your own.

ENERGY CONSERVATION

Because energy can be neither created nor destroyed, it's important to conserve energy when necessary. Imagine a two-story home. Someone leaves a light on in the basement. Nobody goes down there for a week, so they don't see it's on. Everyone agrees the light is using up a lot of unnecessary energy. Everything you focus your energy on is like a different light. Do you have lights being left on you aren't using? Where are you focusing your energy that isn't needed? Are you doing things even though your heart isn't in it? Do you say yes to things because it's too hard to say no?

Conserving energy doesn't mean keeping all your energy to yourself or using it only for self-gain. Conserving energy means using your energy in the right situations—situations that are focused on achieving your goals for the greater good. We discussed that success looks different for everybody. Success might be related to your physical health, mental health, money, or even time. Are you managing and conserving your energy so that it's focused on your definition of success, or are you just expending energy in all of these different areas without any thought?

Knowing when to say "no" means you're practicing energy conservation. It's okay to say no. You don't have to participate in everything you're asked to do. Someone else's passion may not be your own. I've tried adopting other people's passions, and all I end up doing is expending energy I don't have. If it's not congruent with your goals, then don't focus your energy on it. It's better to stay in your lane and concentrate on the things you're passionate about. Remember, you only have so much energy. Conserve it for the things that align with your goals.

Luckily, the more experienced you become, you realize you aren't bullet proof and that conserving energy is a necessity. I have a friend named Bill who is in his mid-forties, runs a successful operation with 40 employees, and recently told me he stopped drinking. But it wasn't because he had a "drinking problem." Rather, he realized how much energy he was expending in the form of time and money to entertain people during happy hours. By no longer drinking, not only is he able to conserve his energy in the form of money saved and direct that energy toward his financial goals, but he also conserves his energy in the form of time spent with the most important people in his life. Make sure you conserve your energy for those things most important to you and don't leave a light on that isn't serving a purpose.

ENERGY WASTE

The opposite of energy conservation is energy waste. Take an inventory of the last 30 days. Be honest: how many times did you spend your money on something you really didn't need? How many times did you eat something you know you shouldn't have? Did you miss out on any opportunities? These are small regrets, but within the bigger picture they are all a waste of energy in some form. Now think about your bigger regrets in life. How much energy did you waste on those?

When you expend energy into something you later wish you hadn't, that energy is gone and you will never get it back. In fact, it takes twice as long to replenish that energy, especially the emotional energy such as sadness, anger, or depression. But rather than dwell on the energy wasted, reflect on why you wasted the energy in the first place. How can you prevent yourself from wasting energy again? When you've made a mistake and wasted energy, it's important to be prepared to make a different choice next time. You want to improve so that you can transfer, recycle, and conserve your energy so that you don't waste it again. That's why it's critical you be able to identify where your energy is flowing at all times.

If you live in a constant state of regret over wasted energy—which can be in the form of complaining that you don't ever have enough time or money—then that in and of itself is a form of wasted energy. It leads to a vicious cycle of shame, embarrassment, and paralyzing you into inaction. It's not easy to admit when we've wasted our time or money, but being aware is the key to preventing it from happening again and moving toward better energy flow and overall energy management.

ENERGY EFFICIENCY

Poor energy management isn't universal. There are people who are very good at managing their energy. They are good collaborators who are mindful of their actions, don't expend unnecessary energy, and are able to influence others through the transfer of energy in a positive way. To be energy efficient is to be respectful of other people's time. Those who are energy efficient are able to focus their flow of energy. They constantly practice how to improve their efficiency as well.

Is there something you do that comes easily or is second nature? Perhaps you have an affinity for numbers and routinely balance your checkbook. Or maybe you're a morning person who enjoys working out before anyone else awakes. Efficiencies are recognized by those tasks you perform by expending the least amount of energy to produce the best outcomes.

Some people seem to always do things the hard way and don't try to improve upon their skills or habits. They do the same thing over and over again expecting different results (which is the definition of insanity). Then they waste their energy by complaining that it doesn't work. We know that complaining not only wastes their energy, but it can waste yours, too. People who are energy efficient are leaders. They are aware of the tasks that need to be done. They are creative, open to ideas, and life-long learners. When somebody who's energy efficient says "Let's go!" everybody follows.

SWITCHING ON/OFF

We all know what it means to be "on." We ramp up our attitude and enthusiasm and expend a large amount of energy to accomplish a task, such as giving a presentation. Being "on" isn't about your behavior; it's about your performance. Being "on" requires physical energy in order to perform at your highest level. When you're asked to deliver on something that requires being "on," you must bring your best performance no matter the circumstances. If I'm asked to present at a speaking engagement, I bring the same amount of energy, focus, and enthusiasm whether there are 400 people or four people attending. Those four people deserve me to be "on" at the same level as the 400 people. You shouldn't change your energy based on the situation.

But we can't always be "on." That's too exhausting. Everybody has to turn that switch off at times. Even the people who seem to always be "on" have to turn it off—that's being human. Knowing when to switch off is a sign of respect to those around you. Have you noticed how people who talk, and talk, and talk drain your energy? Those people who can't turn "off" are being disrespectful of those around them.

Turning it off can happen in many forms. Maybe you just relax and enjoy a theatrical performance or a TV show. Perhaps you turn it off and just listen to someone without interjecting your opinion or advice. Being overly critical is a form of being "on," and it requires practice to be able to sit back, without judgement, and just be a participant. But when you're able to turn it "off," then you can recharge and be ready to focus your energy toward something, and someone, more meaningful that aligns directly with your goals.

UNPLUGGING FROM THE GRID

We discussed earlier that everyone is connected by the power grid, and modern technology and all its conveniences has helped us be connected more than ever. But it has also made life more demanding, immediate, and craving instant gratification. It's made turning "off" even more difficult, because no matter what state or even country you live in, we've all been spoiled by technology.

The media, politics, and millions of products available made available by manufacturers take advantage of our dependence on technology. We've all experienced how much energy we can waste simply by scrolling social media. In fact, it can quickly cause us to short circuit and in extreme cases, lead to an energy crisis and isolation. The only solution is to find times to unplug from the power grid.

Unplugging from the power grid doesn't mean you are doing nothing. Hopefully you take the opportunity to not waste energy and instead do something to develop yourself. Maybe you simply read a book or take a walk. Maybe you work on a hobby or simply declare a pajama day at home. No matter what it is you do, make sure it doesn't involve technology. You may think you're unplugging by watching TV, but that TV is still plugged into the power grid. Truly unplugging means insulating yourself in a way that protects you from the barrage of information via electronic devices.

When we're looking at a device, we become hypnotized and numb to human interaction. We need to be better at putting down our phones and looking up. There's a reason why families enforce rules such as a phone-free dinner table. It's become more difficult to have meaningful conversations as a family. Make sure you are purposely shielding yourself, unplugging from the power grid, and truly connecting with the people around you.

ENERGIZING CONNECTIONS

When people connect, it's one of the most energizing events to witness. Have you ever introduced two people, let them start talking, and there is an explosion of energy right before your eyes? Connecting the right people at the right time is one of the best forms of energy flow. If you become someone who can make energizing connections for others, people will remember you for that. The energy you put into connecting people acts like a battery that energizes them. That energy often comes back to you later, tenfold, and in ways you'd never expect.

As a creator of energizing connections, that energy perpetuates, because we know it's never destroyed. Being a connector is an act of kindness that keeps going from those people to the next and the next. That's why it seems like good people are always connected to other good people. When a bad connection is made, the energy flow is immediately cut off. Whenever I'm new to a group or project, I love making connections and seeing where they go. When a connection is made, you have a level of comfort with that person. That comfortable feeling is actually trust, which is the root of every good relationship.

In business, we ask for referrals. When someone gives you a referral, they expect your connection to be based on trust. Part of that trust relies on transferring energy. If you are purely self-serving and take from the other person—such as not listening to them, or making a hard sell—then you have wasted that connection. Every connection must be earned, otherwise it can turn into a bad connection.

Remember, connections are based on energy. Good energy leads to more good energy. Be purposeful when making connections. Don't just connect people simply to introduce them. Like you, those people only have a finite amount of energy. Be respectful of that by first asking if they think an introduction would be beneficial. If a connection only serves to make you feel better, then it's not an energizing connection. The best connections are the ones that are no benefit to you, but are a benefit to another person or to a cause.

CHAPTER SUMMARY

The entire concept of "let's go" requires energy. It requires an output of stored energy, the energy of others, and being aware of where your energy is flowing. You have to know what kind of energy and the amount of energy you are putting into the world, because others are constantly doing the same to you. Energy is tied to emotion, and if you can't perceive what others are feeling, then you can't identify to whom to transfer your energy.

Every concept in this chapter falls under the umbrella of energy management. You do not want to be an energy resistor, waste your energy to the point of short circuiting, or worse, experience an energy crisis and isolate yourself, or always be "on" and plugged into the grid. Instead, you want to practice being an energy conductor, having an energetic attitude, conserving your energy, which includes knowing when to insulate yourself, switch off, and when to unplug from the power grid, and you want to make energizing connections for others. Doing so will make you so energy efficient that you'll be able to not only go but to keep going and build upon all your successes.

3, 2, 1, Let's Go!

How well do you manage your energy? What areas can you improve?

Are you a conductor or a resistor?

When was the last time you had an energy crisis? Are you able to insulate yourself at times? How often do you unplug from the grid?

How can you make more energizing connections?

NOTES

NOTES

5

HOW TO GO FURTHER

We learn at an early age the concept of "networking." As children, we are expected to network with other students in class, during sports, and other activities—in other words, network with our peers. Networking becomes even more common during our careers, but there is no college class that teaches the art and science of networking. None of my colleagues did their dissertations on networking. Yet it's such a vital component to your growth and success that goes beyond just attending an after-hours mixer where you exchange business cards with other professionals. It's a myth that you have to be an extrovert or outgoing to be good at networking. That's just not true. However, you can't network without giving it much thought otherwise you'll end up with nothing to show for your efforts. In this chapter we'll explore the art and science of proper networking, which requires a balance of value, time, and trust, all with the goal of increasing your social capital. I'll also share a list of dos and don'ts when networking. In order to understand networking, you first must understand your position in the world with regard to the impact you can have.

VALUE

We've discussed how important it is to bring value to others. This is especially true when it comes to networking. Value is always exchanged between two people—it's either taken or given. If value is only being given by one side, then value is lost for the other person. The key to being a successful networker is becoming valuable to others. When that happens, others seek you out, which makes you a trusted ally who is worth their time.

TIME

What is your time worth? Do you say yes to everyone who asks you for a meeting or to join a project? I always felt it was an honor to be asked to a meeting or networking event. After all, I enjoyed having a couple drinks, free appetizers, and socializing. It's easy to get caught up in the glamour of networking. But if you're not providing value, then you'll quickly burn out on networking. Not only does your time have worth, but everyone else's time has worth too. You always need to be respectful of other people's time and not waste it by complaining or revisiting every aspect of your personal life. I will never forget a particular meeting I accepted, and the other person spent the entire time pouring their problems out to me. I looked at my cup of coffee and wondered if I could accidentally spill it on myself so that I'd have to leave. Was a scalding burn worth it? It wasn't, so instead I respectfully said I had another appointment to get to and quickly ended the meeting. But it was a good example of wasting someone's time by providing no value.

How much time should you spend networking? How many events per week should you attend? Should you join your city's chamber of commerce? Should you join a referral group? The amount of time you spend networking depends on the value you bring to it. If you feel like you don't get anything out of networking, it's probably because you're not putting anything into it. If you simply go to events so you can hang out with people you already know, that's socializing, not networking. Are you respecting other people's time at the events, or are you monopolizing it? Time is not a luxury to be spent on things of no value, especially networking.

TRUST

The word "trust" is overused. "Trusted Coach." "Trusted Advisor." Why is the word "trust" needed if the individuals are truly trusted? Trust must be earned and it's only created through observation and interaction. The phrase "look where your feet are pointed" means that what you say and what you do better be one and the same. Trust is the most important ingredient for networking. When you bring value to others and respect their time, then you earn their trust and become someone they want to do business with and network with in return.

SOCIAL CAPITAL

Picture a large pile of cash sitting in front of you. This is your social capital. Every time you come in contact with someone, that cash pile grows either larger or smaller. If you bring value to the interaction, respect their time, and earn their trust, then your pile of cash grows larger. But if you simply talk about yourself, complain, and waste the other person's time, then your pile of cash becomes smaller. You've wasted your social capital. Poor networking is one of the fastest ways to lose your social capital, while proper networking can have a huge impact on your social capital. It's much harder to increase your social capital once you've depleted it, so spend it wisely.

NETWORKING VS. NOTWORKING

Any networking activities you engage in should align with your overall goals. Networking is not a party. You don't get dressed up and make a point to attend a networking event just to hang out with people you see all the time—you can do that outside of a networking event. It's also not an excuse to hand out and collect as many business cards as possible. If this is your experience with networking, then you probably consider it a waste of time and something that has never worked for you. When I first started networking, I thought I had to drink scotch, be incredibly outgoing, and lift my chin when I walked in the door to appear confident. I quickly learned none of that was networking. It was "notworking."

The objective of networking is *not* to have as many two-minute conversations as possible and give away business cards like a human Pez dispenser. You don't even need a business card to network. Your job is to take interest in other people with the goal of making a valuable connection so you can follow up later. There are typically three types of networkers: the wallflower who doesn't want to talk to anybody, the ring leader who lets everyone know they have arrived, and the connector who seeks out people to whom they can bring value. You want to be the third type of networker. In fact, there are three types of connections you should make at every networking event you attend:

1. **Connect with someone you know well.** This is a good connection to start with at an event because it will relax you, especially if you're more of an introvert. It also reinforces the positive relationship you already have established with that person.

But be careful not to spend too much time with them just because you're comfortable. You still need to respect their time. Instead, introduce that person to another connection you know well and then step out of the way and let those two people make their own connection. They will both remember you for it, and it will increase your social capital.

2. **Connect with someone you've only met once or twice.** This is an opportunity to establish the relationship a little further. If there is mutual value, then invite them to a meeting to explore it further. But don't put them on the spot and demand they pull up their calendar. Follow up the next day with a request to meet and be sure to bring value to that meeting.

3. **Connect with someone new.** This can be the most difficult connection to make, but it's easier if you follow a few simple steps. The first is to ask them 2-3 questions about themselves—but don't ask "what do you do?" Jumping right to their job implies that your only interest is in capitalizing on their product or service. We are people first, so take a genuine interest in them before discussing work. If

you take the time to ask questions and listen, the law of reciprocity states they will do the same of you, which fosters value and a good connection for both parties. Good questions to ask them might be, "How are you involved with this organization?" or "How do you know the host?" If for some reason they don't reciprocate and you have a one-sided conversation, then politely move on. But if you feel there's a valuable connection after your conversation, then follow up with them the next day. But do so in a way that leaves an impression, such as a hand-written note stating how much you enjoyed meeting them. Don't ask them for anything. The next time you see them at a networking event, they can serve as the second type of connection for you.

Anyone can participate in networking, but most people end up "notworking." However, if you make these three types of connections at every networking event, then your value, time, and trust from others will increase, and your social capital will grow exponentially.

CAN I DO THIS?

How many times have these thoughts run through your head before an event: "I don't really want to go." "What if I don't know anyone there?" "How long do I have to stay?" "What if someone I don't like is there?" "What if I don't have enough business cards?" All of these thoughts lead to networking paralysis. They are thoughts that come from your inner voice of comfort, and we already discussed that you need to push past that comfort zone in order to grow and succeed. You don't have to be the most outgoing person, the most conversational, or draw the most attention. All you have to do is be authentic and make sure that everything you do aligns with your goals. The world needs all kinds of people—great at speaking, great at humor, great with wit—but it also needs great listeners, and those are the ones who often make the best networkers.

Instead of thoughts related to "can I do this?" change those into thoughts of value. How does this event align with my goals? What value can I bring to the event? Who are the three connections I might be able to make? Being able to answer those value questions will push you past your inner voice of comfort and give you the confidence to make the right decision about whether or not you should spend your precious time at a particular networking event.

NETWORKING DOS AND DON'TS

If you've made the decision to attend a networking event, there are some critical dos and don'ts you need to follow. I've compiled a list of the most common I've experienced during my years of networking.

- **Never act like the smartest person in the room.** Some people don't enjoy networking because they don't think anyone has anything good to offer. Remember, with every interaction, there is something to be learned. The more you listen to others, the smarter you become.

- **Maintain good eye contact.** This is the litmus test as to whether or not somebody is truly listening. If I'm talking to you, I'm focused on you. My eyes aren't scanning the room over your shoulder to see who else just walked in or to find the next person I'm going to talk to.

- **Transition a conversation properly.** If you are having a conversation and someone approaches, it's okay to make them wait. Placing your hand on their shoulder is a good way to acknowledge their presence. Then when there is a pause in the conversation, introduce the person you've been speaking with to the person who is waiting. For example: "Sally Jones, this is Bob Smith. I've known Bob for two years, and he is an avid marathon runner. I've known Sally for five years, and she recently published her first book." That type of positive introduction will boost your social capital with each connection.

- **Don't panic if you forget someone's name.** Don't say, "sorry, I forgot your name." Instead, say, "I'm sure you meet a lot of people, please remind me of your name." You can use the same method if you forget where they work. Then follow up with a good question that re-establishes a positive connection. These situations will actually make you a better networker over time.

- **Your first meeting should not be lunch.** When following up with a connection, don't schedule a lunch meeting, which often requires more than one hour. Instead, be respectful of their time and schedule a meeting at an office—not a coffee shop—and keep it to a maximum of one hour. You can even leverage technology and give them the option for an in-person or video meeting. Also have an agenda for the purpose of the meeting, which includes value you can bring, so that it's not just a "brain picking session" that could waste your time and the other person's time as well.

- **Dress appropriately for the event.** I always dress for success so that I don't ever feel like I need to apologize for what I'm wearing. If you feel out of sync with how you look, it will come across negatively, and you will have a poor experience. It's true that a first impression is a lasting impression, and by dressing professionally, you will also be better remembered for how you communicate, listen, behave, and the value you provide.

- **Don't monopolize someone's time.** Do not talk with just one person the entire event. That's selfish. You need to know when to exit a conservation. Remember, you need to practice the power of three connections in order to create a more valuable network.

- **Exit a conversation politely.** Don't rudely walk away or interrupt the conversation to speak with someone else. If you aren't finding value in the connection or don't want to monopolize someone's time, some simple ways to exit include excusing yourself to get a refreshment, go to the restroom, or to make a phone call to someone you are expecting to meet there.

- **Put away your cell phone.** Do not check your phone or smart watch for texts and emails while you are talking to someone. If someone does that to you, politely say, "That reminds me, I have to follow up with someone as well." You can also wait until another person approaches the conversation, introduce them, and then politely exit if you feel you must check your phone.

- **Always be positive.** We've talked a lot about people who complain. Nobody wants to hear about your shortfalls in life, gossip, or all the challenges you face. This will instantly bankrupt your social capital. Don't tell others you hate networking. If that's the case, then you're doing it wrong and you shouldn't be there. What you say is what you'll be remembered for.

- **How to accept a business card.** When someone hands you a business card, take a minute to study it rather than just stick it in your pocket or purse. Also ask for their preferred method of contact rather than assume it's email versus text.

Everyone is busy, so knowing the best way to get a hold of someone is respectful.

- **Don't overpromise.** There is nothing worse than agreeing to something you have no interest in doing. If you are invited to coffee or lunch on the spot, politely tell them you will be happy to check your schedule and follow up after the event. It's the best way to protect your time and make sure you can truly bring something of value to that connection.

- **How to follow up.** A proper follow-up is one that isn't done in a sales arena. It shouldn't be a meeting to sell a product or service. It should be a meeting in which you provide value in the form of another connection or simply getting to know them better. Remember, networking is all about providing value and business is always the natural result of that.

- **Avoid unconscious rude behavior.** Here are some rude behaviors to avoid, that you may not even realize you're doing:

  1. *Barging in on a conversation*
  2. *Inviting someone to a networking event and not introducing them to anyone*
  3. *Asking condescending questions*

related to money or status

4. *Showing increased interest once you find out their job title*

5. *Assuming occupation based on gender*

6. *Overselling your accomplishments*

- **Network your goals.** Find a networking event or organization that brings out the best in you and your interests and goals. That way, if someone asks how you're connected to the event, you can clearly speak to the organization's mission and its members. It increases your social capital and establishes you as a valuable connection. It also eliminates the thought of whether or not you will get anything of value out of attending.

- **Last to leave.** Never be the last to leave a networking event unless you intend to help clean up. Remember, it's not a party, so don't linger unless you had a role in planning the event in the first place.

- **Network in pairs.** Inviting someone to attend a networking event with you is a great idea. Not only are you providing value by introducing that person to others, but it also takes some of the awkwardness out of walking into an event alone. Just make sure you invite someone who also understands the proper way to network so that you have a shared goal of making an impact.

- **Eating.** Only eat what is served; don't ask for something else. Be mindful of eating while you're having a conversation—please don't try to talk with a mouthful of food, and make sure you have a napkin in your hand.

- **Drinking.** One of the worst things you can do at a networking event is overindulge in alcohol. It's so easy to get caught up in the moment and lose control, especially if the drinks are free. It's neither safe nor professional.

- **Have good hygiene.** This may seem obvious, but some people don't brush their teeth before an event, and bad breath is a barrier and poor reflection on your professionalism. Please also don't chew gum—it's distracting.

- **Proper greeting.** A proper greeting is a simple, firm handshake—not too strong and not too limp. Also use just one hand. Don't place your other hand on top or on their forearm. It's also important to know when to hug someone in greeting and when to refrain. When in doubt, don't hug it out!

Declaring yourself a "hugger" doesn't give you permission to hug the other person.

- **Not a MEET market.** A networking event is not a place to further your dating field (unless it's specifically a singles event). Networking should only be done to further your professional relationships.

- **A connection's spouse.** If one of your connections attends the event with their spouse, acknowledge them with a well-thought-out greeting. For example: "Hi, my name is Jay, and I worked with your husband on the retail development project a year ago." It will help establish trust with them and your connection.

- **Ready body language.** Learn to read faces, body language, and tone of voice. Recognize through visual cues when someone is interested in continuing a conversation or ready to move on. If you can't pick up on small cues, then it can make for a bad experience for everyone. If someone crosses their arms while talking to you or their eyes scan the room, you know it's time to exit the conversation.

- **Don't be a one-upper.** We are a competitive society, but it's okay not to be competitive. Don't try to outdo the other person—if they share how much they sold last month, don't counter by sharing how much you sold. Conversation is most enjoyed when there's a synchronicity or alignment of values.

CHAPTER SUMMARY

The purpose of networking is to help establish you as a valuable influence, both personally and professionally. If you can bring value to the greater good of many, respect their time, and earn their trust, then your social capital will ignite. When that happens, everyone connected to you will follow when you say, "Let's go!"

3, 2, 1, Let's Go!

How much social capital do you have? How can you increase it?

Think back to the last event you attended. What was it? Did you provide value?

Before attending your next event, think about how you can make the three different types of connections. Is there someone you can invite to attend the event with you?

What is your emotional connection to the event?

NOTES

NOTES

6

GO FOR A GOOD REASON

People spend time fantasizing, romanticizing, and visualizing how they want a situation to play out, to the point where it's nothing more than just thinking about something to death. But it doesn't matter how much you want something to happen. What matters is how emotionally connected you are to the outcome. Every time I want to achieve a certain goal, I ask myself, "how does it feel?" As I visualize the outcome, I imagine the words people would use to recognize my accomplishment. I picture how I would walk into a room after achieving my goal. I let myself feel the emotion of how that achievement would impact others. If you take a step back and pay attention to making an impact, then it's easy to tie your goal to an emotion. People are motivated by different things: money, time, fear, and curiosity. You need to find your drivers and what motivates you. The best plans in the world don't matter unless you are emotionally connected to where you want to go. In this chapter we'll examine the different areas of your life where you can make an impact: career, personal, and community. We'll also discuss how to recognize when you've made an impact, what it looks like to others, and what it means to leave a lasting impact or legacy.

MAKING AN IMPACT

If there is no risk with taking action, then there is no reason to move forward. You'd be surprised how many people make goals they aren't emotionally tied to in any way. It's why they fail at them or never attempt to achieve them in the first place. Think back to when you were a kid and really wanted something—a new bike, a basketball hoop, or pair of skates. You told your parents, your friends, your teachers, and even asked Santa. It didn't matter if you were told you couldn't have it or that you had to wait, you were focused and determined to get it. You hadn't yet been conditioned by society to give up when obstacles got in your way. But as adults, when we're told no, or we can't, or obstacles get in our way, we just accept it. Obstacles will pop up every day. You can either accept them, deny them, or fight through them, but you have to choose one—and it better be to fight through them. That's the only way you'll ever make an impact.

Early in my career, I used to dwell on the fact that I never got my college degree. In fact, it haunted me. I knew it was the "right" thing to do and something I was "supposed" to have. When I first started looking for jobs and the requirements included a bachelor's degree, I told myself I just wasn't good enough for that job and for years felt socially inadequate without it. But the reason I never got my degree is because it wasn't my goal. It was my parents' goal and society's goal. The right motivator never presented itself, so I had no emotional connection to it.

Contrast that to three years ago when I first entered the real estate industry and joined my wife's real estate team. I knew that it was a highly competitive field and that many agents don't make it because it's not an easy profession. I declared my goal was to have 40 transactions the first year. A colleague who I respected, politely told me it was impossible, which motivated me to go for it. Being told "no" has always been a driver for me. My first deal was a home listed for $133,000 and located an hour away. I drove there and back 15 times before I finally sold it. The colleague said I was going about it all wrong and wasting my time. Even though I only ended up with 16 transactions that first year, I decided to keep going after my goal. The next year, my wife and I together had 68 transactions totaling $20 million in sales. I had been told I wouldn't make it in real estate, and the emotion behind wanting to succeed became a huge driver in my behavior and my performance. The motivation behind that goal was my emotional connection to it, which is the framework for making an impact in each area of life.

MAKING AN IMPACT IN YOUR CAREER

The word "career" is an old-fashioned term. Your current job or title doesn't define your career. What defines your career is how you act within your profession and whether or not it aligns with your goals. Some people want the work they do every day to be easy. Others enjoy more dangerous professions, such as police officers and firefighters. Life is too short not to do what you love, especially when you spend a majority of your life in a work environment. So, the worst thing you can do in your career is work without being able to do what you want *outside* of work.

If you complain about your job, what exactly are you complaining about? Is it the tasks you perform? Is it that you don't make enough money? Is it that you don't get to make decisions, or have freedom to do what you want because you work at a desk 40-50 hours a week? Actor Arnold Schwarzenegger said, "The day is 24 hours; 6 hours we sleep, so you have left 18 hours, so utilize the 18 hours." In this world of possibilities and opportunities, you can work anywhere you want to. What sacrifices are you willing to make in order to create more opportunities for yourself when you're not at work? If you come up with excuses such as, "I'm too tired," my response is that you're just not inspired.

When career and purpose meet, it creates an impact. I work with real estate agents who are also nurses, teachers, and in law enforcement. They love to do those jobs, but they have also created opportunities outside of those jobs. Real estate is a platform that allows me to use my talents, make my own decisions—and mistakes—and not have to answer to anyone else except the client. It provides me with a freedom to take time to volunteer for causes I'm passionate about. All of those factors contribute to having a career that makes an impact because it aligns with all my goals and allows me to do what I want outside of work.

A career isn't about how much money you can make, it's about how much you can keep in order to achieve your long-term goals. Remember, living a disciplined life—especially with regard to finances—allows you to enjoy a balance and a freedom when you enter retirement. That way, you can continue to enjoy those aspects of life that give you purpose, connection, and drive you emotionally until the day you drop. That's what making an impact in your career is all about.

IMPACT IN YOUR COMMUNITY

It's easy to simply exist within your community. It's another thing to make an impact in it. For example, If you open a small business and it's successful, your entire community is better for it. You provide goods or services that customers need, you provide jobs that help families send their kids to college, and hopefully you support causes that also make the community better. When you put positive influences out into your community and harness the energy of many, that's when you make an impact. It's important not to neglect any one part of your community or leave a void. You must pay attention to every aspect of it. A community works in conjunction—it celebrates, grieves, and rallies together.

Look around your own community. What problems do you notice that you could help solve? What do you want for your community? How does that align with your own goals and talents? I want to help homeless veterans who have post-traumatic stress disorder. But simply writing a check for a cash donation to a veteran's organization doesn't connect me to that cause emotionally. Instead, I immerse myself by participating in an annual 50-mile march to raise money and awareness. I want to feel the physical and mental suffering that those veterans feel, and the march is incredibly challenging both physically and mentally, so it helps me be emotionally connected to the impact. By concentrating on what aligns with your soul, the entire community will be better for it.

But don't focus only on your cause. When others call on you to support their passions in the community, support them. You'd be surprised how little effort it takes to make an impact with so many community organizations. When one individual partners with another individual and so on, it creates a group of supporters that is exponential. The ripple effect is powerful, and often it doesn't cost any money to do it— simply a little time and talent. Our communities give so much to us, we have a responsibility to give back to them. For many people, it was their community that allowed the opportunities for their success. So be sure to give back to it and make an impact.

IMPACT IN YOUR PERSONAL LIFE

I love talking about making an impact in your personal life because it's something I'm always striving to improve. It's the area that is most overlooked and least attended to. When people talk about having a balance between your personal and professional life, I think it's misleading. The more accurate description is that it's a constant prioritization between your personal and professional life. Sometimes you'll prioritize your job. Other times you'll prioritize your kids or marriage. The area that needs your attention the most at any given time is where you will put your energy and make an impact.

I used to think if I worked more hours, I was making a sacrifice for the good of my family that would pay off later. It's the biggest lie I ever told myself. I thought if I prioritized my career all the time, the outcome for my family would be better. Are you trying to earn such a big living that you have no life at home? Years from now your kids won't remember the big sale you made, but they'll remember the baseball game you missed. If you prioritize things in life when they need it, then you won't miss the important moments, and you'll live a happier person. We spend too much of our time seeking frills and thrills instead of enjoying what's right under our own roof.

Making an impact on my children means they are able to problem solve in order to accomplish what they want. I don't have a set path for them to follow. Instead, I teach them the value of time and money. I teach them to solve their way out of or into any situation. I teach them to either develop their own experiences or learn from other people's experiences. All four of my children are so different and have varied personalities and philosophies on life, for which I'm grateful. I hope to have an impact on them in areas they can't learn in a classroom.

Making an impact on my wife means supporting her in the things she wants to do, when she wants to do them. I will always sacrifice my own comfort for her. I try to listen more and give advice less. I want to be part of the family, not dominate the family. Having an impact doesn't have to be a big demonstration. It can be as simple as spending 20 minutes playing catch in the yard with your child. It could be engaging in great conversation at the dinner table. It could be sharing ideas. But in order to make an impact on those in your personal life, don't forget to make yourself a priority too. You can't take care of others and neglect yourself. Making an impact involves everyone in your life—including you.

HOW TO KNOW WHEN YOU'VE MADE AN IMPACT

When you've made an impact in an area of life, there are usually subtle clues. It could be in the form of recognition. Even a simple "thank you" is a small impact. But the largest impacts are the ones that typically go without recognition. Perhaps you've spent time teaching, coaching, or mentoring someone, and after you stopped working with them, you wonder if you really made an impact on them. It might not be until years later that you find out you did, in fact, make an impact. I've had many bosses and mentors over the years who had big impacts on me, and I'm sure many of them never realized it. For example, when I was a young professional, I approached many things with rose-colored glasses. I wanted everyone to be happy, and if they weren't, I thought it was up to me to help them. I had a boss tell me that I was acting like Florence Nightingale, and that I needed to stop trying to fix everyone and not try to always coach people into greatness. I was furious when he said it because I thought he was putting me down. It wasn't until years later I realized he was right. I couldn't fix or help everyone. Instead, I needed to focus my efforts and energy into the places and people where I could make the greatest impact.

A leader's job is not just to create other leaders but to create an environment where others can use their talents autonomously. In fact, the sign a leader has done their job and made an impact is if productivity goes up when the leader isn't present. Telling someone they are doing a good job when they're not isn't helpful. Giving feedback respectfully, even if that truth hurts, makes an impact. If you want to make an impact, expect more out of others and let them know. They will do the same in return. In fact, not only does a good leader impact their team, but the team should also impact the leader. There is no one right way to make an impact. Listening makes an impact. Hugging someone makes an impact. Caring for someone makes an impact. Tough love makes an impact. When you truly make an impact on someone—good or bad, big or small—you will know it.

LEAVING A LASTING IMPACT

At the end of life, people will gather to remember you. It doesn't matter if it's three people or 3,000 people. What's important is this: how do you want to be remembered for making an impact? Do you want to be remembered for making a lot of money? For being the world's best soccer player? For making the best apple pie? I've always wanted to be recorded in history as having done something in history. Maybe it will be a community movement that makes a big impact. No matter what you want to be remembered for, it's only important to you and you alone because ultimately it will affect how you impact the people around you.

Historically, people place an emphasis on leaving wealth to the next generation. If that's true for you, then go one step further—what do you want most for the next generation as a result of your wealth? Do you want them to attend college debt free? Do you want them to be able to start their own business? A legacy is a forever impact that lives on for many generations, such as a memorial, foundation, or even a memoir that gets passed down. The stronger your legacy, the bigger the impact you'll make for generations. Your legacy can live on through the work you did to make an impact, through your teachings, and through the people you've mentored through life who carry on your practices. So, think about your lasting impact and prepare and execute it so that you have a true legacy.

CHAPTER SUMMARY

The only way to "let's go" is if you are emotionally tied to the outcome of what it is you are going after. This is why it's so important to make sure that your goals are clear and tied to what success means for you and for the greater good. When you focus your energy on your priorities, that's when you start making an impact—on your career, your community, and your personal life. The greatest rewards come from impacting others and have a ripple effect that lasts for generations.

3, 2, 1 Let's Go!
How can you make an impact in your

career? What changes do you need to make in order to have the freedom to pursue your goals outside of work?

How can you make an impact in your community? What is a change you'd like to see, and how can you use your talents to help?

How can you make an impact in your personal life? Are you able to prioritize what needs your attention and energy?

Write down three things for which you'd like to be remembered. What can you do now to prepare to leave that legacy? What teachings and practices can you share that will leave a lasting impact?

NOTES

NOTES

7

MOTIVATING OTHERS TO GO

The phrase "Let's go" means nothing if nobody will listen to you. You can have the biggest megaphone, yelling to a crowd of strangers to follow you, and they will stare at you like you're crazy. Why? Because you haven't provided them with any value that would lead to their trust in you. It's actually not accurate to say one person can motivate another. Instead, what motivates someone is their buy-in, or belief in you. When people buy into what they can't see, it's called trust, which is at the core of motivating others to "go." I believe there is an energy that surrounds every person. When you put that energy out into the world, you get it back in a different form. We discussed the concept of social capital earlier. When you provide value, which increases your social capital, then people put their trust in you because it's right for them or the people who surround them. When you add value, they will truly follow you.

Having people who trust you means you're a leader, and being a good leader involves having excellent communication skills. You don't have to be eloquent or studious, but you do have to be able to speak up, and then be able to stop talking and listen. I can't stress the importance of active listening. When it comes to problem solving, the more we talk, the greater the chance we're trying to solve a problem that doesn't even exist. Instead, we should ask questions such as, "Tell me more about that," "What do you think we should do?" "What outcome would you like to see?" You have to shut your mouth in order to be engaged in active listening.

Earlier we discussed that being a good leader means you have to quickly assess a situation, recognize verbal and nonverbal clues, and make tough decisions if it's for the good of many. You also have to be brutally honest and own up to any outcome. No matter your title or position, you can be a leader as long as you bring value. If you want to lead, you can. But you can only lead something that you are emotionally tied to so that others can see the value you bring and buy in to your call to follow.

SEEK FEEDBACK

Most people want to be in charge of something, but it's not always glamorous. There are leaders who bang their head against the wall because people don't respond—they haven't bought in to their leader. It's important to remember that human beings want to be comforted, cared for, and to feel safe. If they don't feel those basic needs are being met, then they won't respond the way you want them to—they won't trust you. If you put yourself first and your people second, they will feel that. A group must feel comfortable enough to share their ideas, otherwise there is no reason for them to be present.

As leaders, we need to be highly aware of our actions and the balance of input and output with a group of people. Sometimes leaders think they are doing everything correctly, but they aren't getting the results they want. In that case, it's time to stop thinking and start asking—it's amazing what you find out simply by asking for feedback. Usually, the leader is surprised to learn why things aren't working. A leader doesn't have to come up with all the ideas, they just have to orchestrate the group and then rely on them to execute. It's no different than the conductor of a symphony. Imagine if in in the middle of a piece, the conductor decided the brass section didn't sound right and ran up to a tuba player and took over—it would disrupt every musician and ruin the piece. Instead, the conductor finishes the piece and discusses the problem with the brass section later—asking for everyone's feedback. The best answers always come from the group you are leading.

SHOW YOU CARE

The idea of feeling cared for by a leader is so critical to having everyone's buy-in. Want to motivate others? Show genuine interest in people. Get to know their family members, hobbies, and passions. Write them hand-written notes. Send flowers if they're sick. Give their child a card when they graduate from high school. When a leader lacks the ability to motivate, it's usually because they lack compassion. If the leader doesn't care about their people, they won't care about the leader. Productivity, trust, and buy-in all go up when people observe a leader who truly cares.

OWN YOUR MISTAKES

If you want others to believe in you, own your mistakes, no matter how much it hurts. And it will hurt. But you will also learn and rise from those mistakes. A good leader prepares for setbacks. That doesn't mean being cautious or not taking risks. It means having a resolution process in place so that you can quickly identify and own any mistake that's made. In a group setting, every mistake should be owned by the leader. To quote the song "Dream On" by Aerosmith: "You got to lose to know how to win." A good leader is responsible for steering the ship, and you must be vulnerable and transparent, and ask for forgiveness.

When I first joined my wife's real estate team, I

thought I could incorporate the same techniques I had used in a prior sales position and would be highly successful. I wanted to recruit more agents so that we'd generate more income. To me, it was all about the sales cycle. I was like a bull in a china shop, unleashing my ideas on everyone all at once. I was a fast and furious recruiting machine. What I didn't realize was that real estate isn't about transactions. It's a highly emotional sale that relies on the interactions between the transactions. It's about the 99 things that happen between looking at a home and receiving the keys. I tried to simply create an environment that I thought would create more dollars. I failed miserably, and it took me 18 months to realize it. We even lost a few agents along the way.

I finally admitted to the team that I was wrong, and it wasn't easy to admit I'd made a mistake. I had only been focused on money and growth of the recruiting machine I had tried to create. I lost sight of the most important aspect—the people. The team accepted my apology by sharing their own ideas for growth that focused on quality, not quantity. When you admit your shortfalls, people see you as human, and you're more relatable. The biggest mistake a leader can make is wanting others to think they are infallible. A true leader will be harder on themselves than anyone else. Remember, a setback is nothing but a setup for a comeback!

CHAPTER SUMMARY

When you try to motivate others and find it's not working, usually it's not their fault, it's yours. Anyone can be a leader, but to be a good leader, you must be a good communicator. Strong communication skills require knowing when to speak up and then knowing when to stop talking and listen. If you aren't receiving buy-in from your team, then it's time to start asking questions and requesting their feedback. Let them openly share ideas. A good leader also genuinely cares for the people with whom they work. When someone feels cared for, then they feel valued, and that feeling is reciprocated. Finally, good leaders take responsibility for mistakes. They have a process to quickly resolve them that includes asking for input. Owning up to mistakes shows a vulnerability that people respect. It brings the trust and buy-in full circle, so when you say, "Let's go!" people follow.

3, 2, 1, Let's Go!

Do you regularly ask your team for feedback? Are they comfortable sharing their ideas with you?

When is the last time you asked someone on your team about their family? About their hobbies? Made a personal gesture toward them?

Think back to a mistake you made. Did you own up to it? Did you apologize to your team for it?

NOTES

NOTES

8

3, 2, 1, LET'S GO!

Every concept we've discussed throughout this book comes down to one thing: mindset. But it's an elusive concept that many people don't know how to apply to themselves. Yet when you wake up every single morning, you are governed by your mindset. Think of it as your own operating system. It's not just a measure of how you feel. It's the habits you default to when things get tough—a set of rules you fall back on. Your mindset will always be the loudest voice in the room. It's your attitude, posture, and behavior that governs every decision you make and every situation you encounter. It sets you up for either success or failure. Make sure your mindset is strong because there will be headwinds, especially when you are trying to improve and grow. People will say things to you such as, "You're perfect just the way you are." "Don't be so hard on yourself." "I wish I had your life." These are all subtleties that can get in the way of your own growth and hold you back from being able to "go."

A WORRYING MINDSET

A strong mindset starts with strong mental health. Anxiety and worry play a part in everyone's life, some more than others. Worrying causes such a strong burden, it may paralyze you or make you give up in life. We worry ourselves to death. We worry about things to worry about. We worry based on past traumatic experiences. We are conditioned to worry. Can you imagine if a stunt person worried about every stunt they performed? The reason they don't is because they have learned that with preparation, they know they will successfully perform the stunt. Their career would be short-lived if they worried each time. Does a person recovering from a heart attack worry about what they are wearing when someone comes to visit? Does a parent worry about a child's messy room when the child finally arrives home after being late?

Most of the things we worry about never even come to fruition, so all that anxiety is unnecessary, robbing us of our happiness and paralyzing us into inaction. Here's an exercise I want you to do:

1. Think about the last three things you worried about and write them down.
2. Beside each one, write down the outcome that worried you, such as displeasing

someone, making the wrong decision, failing, etc., and the feelings associated with it. This might include fear, insecurity, or lack of control.

3. Next, write down the actual outcome and the feelings you had as a result, which might be increased confidence or reassurance.

4. Repeat this exercise over the course of several days every time you have a worry.

Did worrying end up making an impact on the outcome? The answer is usually no. You'll quickly start to see a pattern that most things you worry about never even happen, and very few worries are actually valid. A majority of worries just aren't worth your time, energy, or effort.

Having a strong, laser-focused mindset helps prevent worrying from getting in the way of your goals. It also helps prevent you from succumbing to unwanted advice. When friends or family warn you against failure, a strong mindset will act as a barrier, allowing you to keep your distance and protect yourself from those unfounded worries. Remember, there is a difference between advice that has no basis in experience and advice from someone who has achieved what you want to achieve. Only take advice from the latter. You need to plant your flag in the ground and claim your mindset instead of letting it blow in the wind and accepting that whatever comes along is good enough. If you simply take each day on as it comes, you'll never be able to grow and achieve your goals.

UNIVERSAL TRUTH

None of the concepts in this book will work unless you find a way to connect them emotionally to your mindset. This will just be another book that sits on the shelf. But if you choose to embrace even a few of the concepts, it could dramatically change your life. Some of you may have hit rock bottom, and others may just be facing a challenge. It doesn't matter what level of life you're in, you have to acknowledge the obstacles facing you and realize that *you* probably put those obstacles there. The number one universal truth in life is that you reap what you sow. In other words, what you put out into the world comes back to you. Whatever you plant and nurture will grow and produce an outcome, either good or bad. In order to make sure the outcome is positive, you have to make sure the language you use is positive as well. Feeding your brain with positive influences comes in a number of forms. Here are some universal truths I've discovered help people achieve their goals:

I. **Model your behavior after someone who has accomplished something similar to your own**

goal. If you haven't experienced the outcome, then you should study the behavior of someone who has. This person could be an actual mentor, or just someone you consider to be successful and want to borrow from their experience. Don't model your behavior after someone who has no experience in the outcome you desire.

2. **Invest in a coach.** There are all types of coaches who offer services, both business and personal or life coaches. A coach provides value by helping you identify shortfalls and how to work through them. When you invest in a coach, it helps keep you accountable because you're buying in to their experience and the outcomes they've helped others produce—many of which are similar to the outcome you want to achieve.

3. **Watch videos online.** We are visual animals, and there are so many great resources online. You can find videos and webinars on any topic that can help feed your brain and give you language for a positive mindset.

4. **Listen to podcasts.** The rise of podcasts has proven to be such a valuable tool. It's so easy to listen to a podcast while doing another activity, such as driving,

cleaning, or exercising—any activity that puts you in a mental state where you are open to new ideas. Just like with online videos, there is a podcast for every interest. I've found that some of my best ideas have come while I'm behind the steering wheel of my car, listening to a podcast.

5. **Read, read, read.** When you read, you can't think or worry about anything else. You should read books by people who've experienced what you want to accomplish. You should read about things that make you feel good. You should read about anything that fills your mind with positive thoughts and strengthens your mindset. Make reading a part of your disciplined daily routine.

6. **Examine your own successes and failures.** It's important to take inventory of your own struggles and triumphs. What did you do to get those outcomes, both good and bad? It's easy to take inventory of our successes, but when something bad happens, we tend to dwell on it and not learn from it. Instead of unpacking your bags in that dark place full of self-pity, determine what actions and behavior you did to produce that unfavorable outcome, and then move on so that you know what to

do in order to have a better outcome next time.

7. **Develop a routine.** We talked about how important it is to be disciplined and establish good habits. The last time you implemented a new habit, how did you do it? I doubt you started 10 new habits at once. If you were to add one small, new habit to your morning routine, what would it be? Maybe it's reading something inspirational for 10 minutes while you drink your cup of coffee. Maybe it's 10 minutes of exercise. Maybe it's spending 10 minutes in meditation or gratitude. Even a simple habit can increase an outcome exponentially as long as it's directly tied to that outcome.

8. **Get physical.** It doesn't matter if you enjoy yoga, running, walking, hiking, or CrossFit, you have to move—in whatever way you can. Once it becomes part of your routine, then try doing a little more. When you push yourself physically, even just a little, it will have positive results for both your body and mind.

All of these activities will go a long way toward feeding your brain and body, which will ultimately strengthen your mindset. When combined with positive self-talk, it will set you up for success.

SELF-TALK

The language you use inside your head is self-talk. It's always louder than anyone else's voice. It's the last thing you hear before going to bed and the first thing you listen to when you wake up. It's the voice you hear before taking action. It is passive and always turned on. You can't ignore it, but you can control it. Self-talk is critical to your success. It dictates your daily routine. Whatever you tell yourself will happen, usually does. The conversation you have with yourself usually takes place in an instant. For example, before walking into a room full of people, the following thoughts might flash inside your mind: "What if they don't like me?" "What if I don't fit in?" "Is this going to be a waste of time?" You can dwell on that negative self-talk without even realizing it's happening. Compare that to the following: "I'm going to be myself." "I'm comfortable in my own skin." "I enjoy learning from others." "I'm going to meet like-minded people." That language is much different and will lead to more confidence, a better experience, and ultimately a more successful outcome.

What do you say to yourself as soon as you wake up every morning? Some people immediately dread the day and think about how tired they are, how much they have to get done, and how they don't feel like going to work. Others spring out of bed, excited to jump start their day. Why do you say the things you do first thing in the morning? Who taught you to think that way? Where does the voice originate? It usually comes from your environment, the people you pay the most attention to, and the activities you engage in—all of it shapes your self-talk. In order to improve or change your self-talk, you must first acknowledge what it is you're saying to yourself and then take responsibility for it. Nobody controls the voice inside your head except you.

Most people make things harder than they need to be. You will meet many challenges, but you are no different than anyone else in facing those challenges and dealing with them. You can choose to be a victor or a victim. When going through a growth stage in life, we tend to use language in our self-talk that makes us feel like victims who have no control over life. But simply by changing your language, you can drastically change your self-talk. Here are some examples of victor versus victim self-talk:

1. **"I'm sacrificing so much."** Instead try saying, "I'm taking advantage of an opportunity." When we give things up in order to work on a project or ourselves, such as going out with friends, we associate that with sacrifice. But that self-talk is sabotaging because it disregards the bigger picture, which is meeting a goal you set out to accomplish.

2. **"I'm hustling so hard."** Instead try

saying, "I'm putting in the necessary work to get the outcome I want." The word "hustle" has come to be associated with showing up for work, returning phone calls, and attending countless meetings. But when I hear the word "hustle," I picture a coal miner in the early 1900s, working underground 18 hours a day for pennies on the dollar. To me, that's true hustle. The next time you hear someone say, "I'm hustling," ask what they mean by it. Chances are good they're using it incorrectly.

3. **"Getting what I want is so painful."** Instead try saying, "I'm doing what's necessary to improve my habits." When people try to improve their physical and mental health, they often have to follow rigid rules that can cause some degree of pain and suffering, both mentally and physically depending on what they're trying to improve. But what they are really doing is creating a repeatable system of habits to get them to a better place.

It's so important to examine your self-talk. Champions don't wake up and wonder how their day is going to go. They know what will happen because they use positive language from the moment they wake up. They also have disciplined habits in place. And if something unexpected comes up, they have the confidence to move through that obstacle. Self-talk is a skill that must be developed just like any other skill. You can't change it in just one day. You have to practice your self-talk every single day. You can self-talk yourself into despair or you can self-talk yourself into success. It's easy to have positive self-talk when everything is going great. The better skill is to catch yourself saying something negative and turning it around before it affects your mindset. When you have a positive self-talk and a strong mindset, you can achieve anything. When you're in that mental state—or zone—you need to examine your thoughts and behavior so you can sustain it. People never question why things go right, they only focus on things that go wrong. Just like you can get stuck in a dark place, you can also get stuck in a great place. And if you know what actions you took to get there, then you can ride that wave and maintain direction to achieve your goals.

TAKE ACTION NOW

If you're ready to start your journey, here are three steps you can take today:

1. **Admit the current state you're in.**
   Tell yourself the truth about where you're at in your growth process. Write down what you want to achieve and everything that is holding you back. For example,

instead of saying, "I'm unhappy with my health," go deeper and identify exactly what it is you're unhappy with. Is it your weight? Do you have a bad back? Do you lack energy? Be very specific. Being honest with yourself is difficult because it means having to admit failure, but it's the only way to start to grow. If you aren't sure what to write down, start asking yourself questions such as, "What do I want for my family?" "What do I want in my career?" "Am I happy with my finances?" "Do I need to add or eliminate someone from my tribe?" You will quickly identify the area that is most important to you.

2. **You can't address everything at once.** Once you've identified the one or two things that are most important, lean into them. Write them down someplace where you will see it every day, such as your bathroom mirror. I've posted my goals to the bathroom mirror many times. It will become part of your disciplined daily routine for self-talk. One of my goals was to deepen my relationships to create stronger bonds with people I care about. I wrote this down, posted it to my bathroom mirror, and made it part of my morning self-talk each day. When I encountered someone important to me, I made a point to ask a

personal question about their spouse, children, a vacation they recently took, or some other aspect of their life. At first it felt a little awkward, but the more I did it, the more natural it felt. I received great feedback—they thanked me for asking and gladly told me about their family while I listened. I didn't do it with everybody, I only concentrated on those people with whom I wanted to improve my relationship, and it has been rewarding in so many ways.

3. **Be intentional.** Whatever you decide to work on, practice it every single day. Be relentless about it. Some of you will develop the habit quickly, and others will take a longer time to develop it as part of a routine. Nobody learns a habit overnight. What comes naturally to you may not come naturally to others. Improvement isn't easy, especially when you're trying to create a better version of yourself. For example, if you want to have more patience, how do you intentionally practice that? One simple way is to pick the longest check out line at the grocery store. Nothing will teach you patience faster than that! Take it one step further by letting someone else go in front of you. Tell yourself it doesn't matter if it takes five or

ten extra minutes to checkout, and then relax. Have a friendly conversation with someone else waiting in line. No matter what your goal is, find ways to be intentional so that you can practice the skills necessary to move you closer to accomplishing it.

CHAPTER SUMMARY

We are what we think. Our mindset paves the way for everything we do and is our default when things get tough. So much of our mindset is dictated by our self-talk, which begins the moment we wake up every day. We need to remember the universal truths that successful people follow in order to model after those who have experienced the same outcomes we desire. Whether from a mentor, coach, podcast, or book, feeding your mind with positive thoughts cultivates positive self-talk. In other words, feeding your brain feeds your mindset, so make sure you're feeding it positive input for a positive outcome.

When you look back on the achievements you've already had in life, they weren't accomplished instantly or even in just one step. You were intentional, with a strong, disciplined mindset, and you went after your goal every single day. You don't have to try to do every concept in this book—just take one step. Everything you need is already inside of you. The next time you run into a problem, challenge, or major life goal you want to achieve, remember that it all starts with the one phrase that can change your life. "Let's go!"

3,2,1, Let's Go!

What is something you worried about recently? Did it actually happen? How many of the things you worry about actually play out?

How strong is your mindset? What can you do to make it stronger?

What is something negative you tell yourself? How can you turn it around into a positive?

What is one small goal you can take action on today? Let's Go!

NOTES

NOTES

ABOUT THE AUTHOR

Jay Miralles was born first generation in San Francisco, California, after his parents arrived in America. He watched his immigrant parents work hard to support their family. Their actions and life lessons shaped who he is today. He learned first-hand how his parents' work ethic allowed them to move from a basement in the Avenues to a middle-class suburb. As a teenager, he struggled in school with average grades and was easily bored with the norm or status quo.

Jay questioned everything. He realized his independence was so important, he enlisted in the Air Force at the age of 17. His love for country grew rapidly, and he realized many things people take for granted. His deployment to places such as Alaska, Germany, and Saudi Arabia, and more, shaped his perspective on how the world is connected. After ten years in the Air Force, he decided to move to Omaha, Nebraska.

Some of the early jobs that gave him valuable experience included ten years in radio, a background in information technology, and teaching at a local college. He also co-founded three professional networking organizations. Eventually, he found a niche in insurance/financial services and real estate. He quickly excelled in sales, which led to coaching and leadership positions.

His background has prepared him well to speak on stage, conduct podcasts, author articles, and serve as a go-to for interviews. His passion is more than just inspiring people; it's working closely with individuals and organizations to help identify the opportunities for them to make the best impact.

Jay and his wife Becky are blessed with four children: Aubrey, Jade, Jordan, and Mason. They have a German Shepard named King and a Pekingese Shih Tzu Poodle mix, Chewy, who thinks he is the same size as King. They all call Nebraska, home.

www.letsgo321.com